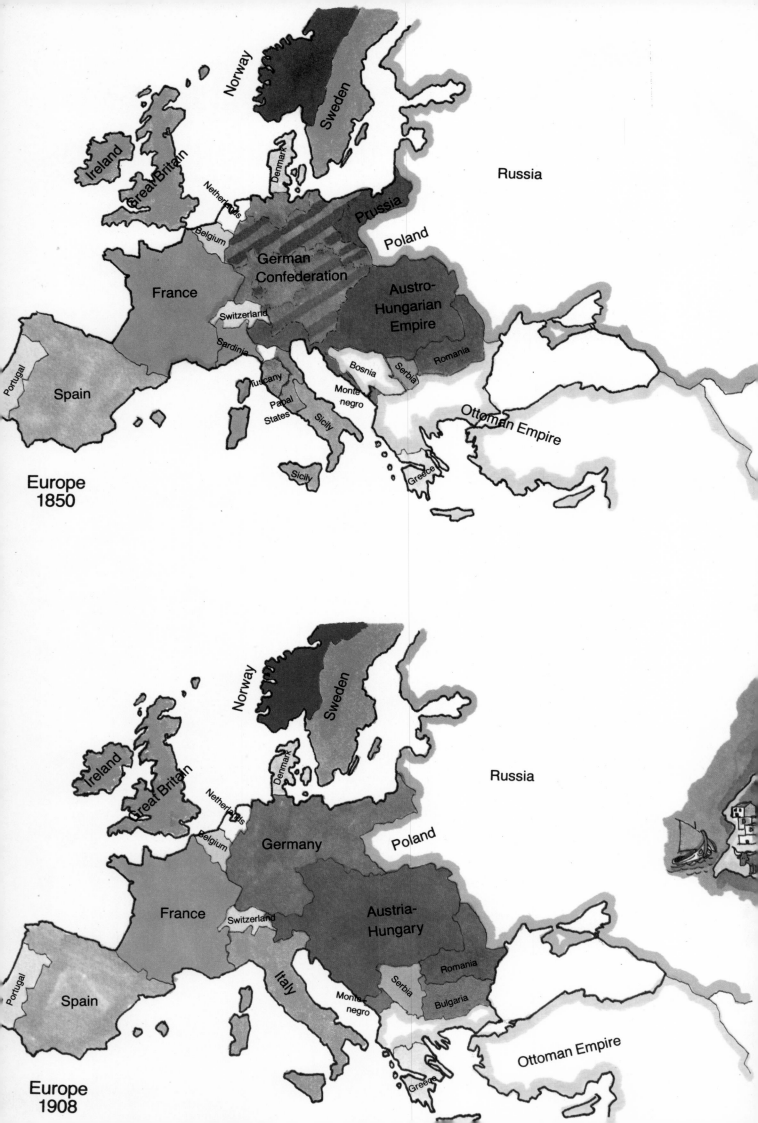

Europe
1850

Europe
1908

The Church and the Modern Nations

An Illustrated History of the Church

Created and Produced by Jaca Book

The First Christians
From the beginnings to A.D. 180

The Church Established
A.D. 180–381

The End of the Ancient World
A.D. 381–630

The Formation of Christian Europe
A.D. 600–900

The Middle Ages
A.D. 900–1300

**The Church
in the Age of Humanism**
A.D. 1300–1500

Protestant and Catholic Reform
A.D. 1500–1700

The Church in Revolutionary Times
A.D. 1700–1850

The Church and the Modern Nations
A.D. 1850–1920

An outline by chapter can be found on the last two pages of this volume.

The Church and the Modern Nations

An Illustrated History of the Church

From 1850 to 1920

Translated and adapted by John Drury
Illustrated by Franco Vignazia

Winston Press   430 Oak Grove   Minneapolis, Minnesota 55403

Published in Italy under the title
La chiesa le guerre e i regimi: La chiesa e la sua storia
Copyright © 1979 Editoriale Jaca Book.

**Licensed publisher and distributor
of the English-language edition:**
 Winston Press, Inc.
 430 Oak Grove
 Minneapolis, Minnesota 55403
 United States of America

Agents:
Canada—
 LeDroit/Novalis-Select
 135 Nelson St.
 Ottawa, Ontario
 Canada K1N 7R4

Australia, New Zealand, New Guinea, Fiji Islands—
 Dove Communications, Pty. Ltd.
 Suite 1, 60–64 Railway Road
 Blackburn, Victoria 3130
 Australia

United Kingdom, Ireland, and South Africa—
 Fowler-Wright Books, Ltd.
 Burgess St.
 Leominster, Herefordshire
 England

Created and produced by Jaca Book, Milan
Color selection: Mediolanum Color Separations
Printing: Gorenjski tisk, Kranj

History Consultant: The Rev. Marvin R. O'Connell
                Professor of History, University of Notre Dame
Winston Staff: Florence Flugaur, Cyril A. Reilly—editorial
            Chris Larson—design

Library of Congress Catalog Card Number: 78-67839
ISBN: 0–86683–159–2

5   4   3   2   1

An Illustrated History of the Church

The Church and the Modern Nations

Introduction

Perhaps the clearest difference between our times and earlier centuries is the swiftness with which things now change. This has been true especially since about 1850, the date at which this volume picks up the history of the Church. Developments in politics, economic systems, science, work, social relationships, and leisure have all been so rapid that they still bewilder us.

In any event Christians who lived from the middle of the nineteenth century to the end of the first World War and who, like Christians at all times, believed in changeless truth and enduring values had to adjust their faith and practice to the fact of change. Many of them, like Pope Pius IX, did so by vigorously condemning the errors they thought were part of the modern developments. Others, like Pope Leo XIII, tried to find ways to accommodate the new ideas to the old faith. Still others—lonely thinkers like Kierkegaard and Newman—examined from new angles the kind of commitments Christians should make in the modern world which presented such a mixture of good and evil: a world which produced enormous new wealth, which tried harder than ever before to remove human suffering and ignorance, which was more sensitive than ever before to the political rights of individuals; and yet a world which more deeply than ever before exploited people, which created industrial wastes and vast new slums, which was guilty of the most awful violence.

The challenges to Christians during this era were many and profound. Most profound of all perhaps was the realization that the modern world could be Christian only to the extent that Christians themselves were prepared to give witness to their faith.

Marvin R. O'Connell

1. In 1848 Italian
revolutionaries began a drive
to unify Italy and tried
to take over the papal
territory. Pope Pius IX
fled from Rome but
returned in 1850,
protected by French
soldiers. He tried
to reassert the authority
of the pope and to make
Rome a real center
for Roman Catholicism.
In 1854 he proclaimed
the dogma of the
Immaculate Conception
of Mary.

When Pius IX became pope in 1846, he impressed many people very favorably. He was friendly, and he seemed open to change and reform. He gave many papal audiences and clearly wanted to improve the condition of the Papal States. (The Papal States were a region in Italy belonging to the Church and ruled by the pope.)

Many Italians expected Pius IX to support efforts to free Italy from the control of Austria and France and to create a more united country. Some Italians wanted to form a fed-

eration of Italian states under the presidency of the pope. Others, including Mazzini and Garibaldi, wanted a democratic republic. This would mean revolting against Austria, driving out ruling princes, and depriving the pope of the Papal States.

Uprisings in France and Austria early in 1848 helped to spark revolts in Milan and Venice. Other sections of Italy, including the Papal States, sent troops to aid the rebels. Radicals in Rome, led by Mazzini and Garibaldi, proclaimed a republic, and an alarmed Pius IX fled to Gaeta for safety. Austria soon put down the uprisings in its Italian territories, and French troops came to restore the pope to power in Rome. On April 12, 1850, Pius IX returned to Rome, protected by French soldiers. These new trends in public life made Pope Pius IX and many other European rulers fearful. They were convinced that firm resistance to new ideas was necessary so that their well-ordered world would not fall into chaos. Pius IX believed that it was his duty as pope to stand firm against radical ideas which could undermine religious doctrine and could use violence to endanger legitimate rule. He also believed that the Papal States were essential to the papacy because only in being a ruler himself could the pope guarantee his religious independence.

Pius IX wanted to strengthen papal authority and make Rome a center of Roman Catholic life and government. Seminarians from other countries were encouraged to study in Rome, where new colleges were established for Latin Americans, Poles, North Americans, and Irish. Pius IX also fostered the growth of the Catholic press. In 1861, he encouraged the beginning of *L'Osservatore Romano (The Roman Observer)*, a newspaper that is now the semi-official newspaper of the Holy See.

During the 1800s, devotion to Mary the Mother of Jesus had been growing among Roman Catholics. In 1830, Catherine Labouré, a French nun, had a vision of Mary. Catherine reported that Mary had asked that a medal be made with her picture engraved on it and with the following prayer around the edge: "Mary conceived without sin, pray for us..." "Conceived without sin" meant that Mary had been preserved by God's grace from original sin from the very first moment of her life in her mother's womb. This belief was a long-standing tradition among Roman Catholics, though some theologians had not accepted it.

Pope Pius IX, who had a deep devotion to Mary, decided to ask the Catholic bishops of the world what they thought about the doctrine. Their response was overwhelmingly favorable, so in 1854 Pius IX, supported by the findings of a theological commission, officially proclaimed the dogma of the Immaculate Conception. Besides helping to encourage devotion to Mary among Catholics, this action was a strong assertion of the pope's authority in the Catholic Church.

2. People's work and living conditions during the 1800s in Europe were greatly affected by scientific discoveries, inventions, and the ongoing Industrial Revolution. These factors greatly influenced people's ideas about God, religion, traditional beliefs, and the role of the Christian churches.

Important changes in outlook took place in Europe during the 1800s. Scientific discoveries, inventions, and the ongoing Industrial Revolution were affecting people's work and their living conditions. New theories about the age of the world and the origin of living things raised questions about biblical accounts and traditional beliefs. To people favoring popular government, some Christian churches seemed to be tied too closely to outmoded forms of government and to aristocratic ruling classes. If new economic and political approaches were to be successful, the forces of the old order and backwardness would have to be disregarded or openly attacked and defeated. And then there were more radical ideas suggesting that there was no God at all (atheism), or that the question of God's existence did not matter since we could never know the answer for sure anyway (agnosticism).

It is not surprising that the various Christian churches felt they were under attack, for they were, in more than one respect. But many of the attacks had to do with traditional ways of thinking rather than actual beliefs, and it was possible to counterattack by rethinking one's position and examining other viewpoints carefully. That was not done very often in the nineteenth century. There was little discussion between people of opposing viewpoints on religion or on other matters.

The Roman Catholic Church, for example, had come down hard on liberal Catholics in France during the 1830s. After 1848 liberal ideas of all sorts were treated harshly by Pope Pius IX. In return, Europeans favoring newer and more liberal views tried to push the Church out of sight altogether. The illustration on these pages is one way of symbolizing what went on. A father is trying to let his son see and examine new ideas and discoveries about human life. But he also wants his son not to be influenced by "outmoded" ideas and practices, so he is having certain religious themes and scenes removed from his display case at home.

In the following paragraphs, we will consider a few of the new ideas that were circulating at the time. In *The Essence of Christianity* (1841) Ludwig Feuerbach asserted that religious feelings and ideas about God were really human feelings and qualities. Feuerbach said that human beings attributed their own hopes and ideals to an imaginary being called God. Instead of doing this, he said, human beings should focus on themselves and on nature, of which they are a part, and develop their capabilities as much as possible. Religion was simply "the dream of the human mind," according to Feuerbach. His views influenced many in Germany and elsewhere, including young Karl Marx. Marx went on to challenge traditional views about social and economic life, while other German readers of Feuerbach and Hegel questioned the reality of Jesus and the historical truth of biblical texts.

In France, Auguste Comte (1798–1857) developed a "Positive Philosophy" that was widely influential. There were three stages of intellectual development in human history, said Comte. In the theological stage (which

attempted to explain the world in religious terms), human beings attributed everything to supernatural beings. In the metaphysical stage (which attempted to explain the world simply by thinking about it in general terms), they explained everything by appealing to abstract forces, such as Nature. In the third and final stage, the stage of Comte's Positive Philosophy, however, they would combine reason with down-to-earth observation to establish connections between things observed and general facts. Then, Comte thought, belief in humanity as the Great Being would replace belief in God.

In England, Charles Darwin published his *The Origin of Species* in 1859. This book, based on both on his theories and his research, did more to spread the scientific theory of evolution than any previous work had done. *The Origin of Species* caused an uproar in religious circles because it seemed to cast serious doubt on biblical accounts of creation (Genesis 1 and 2) and on the notion of divine creation. Most people understood the Bible to mean that all the animals on earth had been created by God in exactly the same form as they are in today. According to Darwin's theory, present-day forms of animals seem to have developed through chance and the survival of the fittest. In 1871, Darwin extended the theory of evolution to humanity in his book *The Descent of Man*. Bitter debate about Darwin's work still goes on today.

3. In 1843 Sören Kierkegaard of Denmark began to publish his thoughts about religion. He said that belief in Christ's divinity called for total and unquestioning obedience to God. Kierkegaard claimed that Christian churches did not teach true Christianity.

One of the more isolated but brilliant figures in the history of modern religious thought was Sören Kierkegaard. He was born in Copenhagen, Denmark, in 1813. His father was a successful businessman tormented by religious doubts and fears. The boy's religious upbringing was strict and serious. He later complained that he had never had a real childhood or friends to play games with.

In 1830 Kierkegaard went to study theology at the University of Copenhagen, since his father wanted him to become a minister. There he read in a wide variety of subjects, practiced his fine debating skills, and enjoyed the typical pleasures and pastimes of university students. As a result, it took him ten years to get his degree.

In 1843, Kierkegaard settled down in the home his father had left him and published a book called *Either/Or.* He devoted the rest of his life to thinking and writing. In *Either/Or,* he described the esthetic stage and also the ethical stage of life. People in the esthetic stage, he said, lived from moment to moment, seeking immediate pleasure according to their own whims. People in the ethical stage accepted duty as a natural part of life.

Kierkegaard had deep feelings of anxiety and guilt. He wondered if a series of griefs in his family might not be signs of divine displeasure. Because of these feelings, Kierkegaard reacted sharply against the philosophy of Hegel, which was very influential in Denmark. Unlike Hegel, Kierkegaard thought that the universe was not a nice, reasonable place where one could calmly find a place for everything: the world, nature, humanity, and God. One had to make choices, hard choices: *either* this *or* that. In the religious stage, he

said, the human individual faced God, the Wholly Other, the unknown Absolute, in a state of fear and trembling. The search for truth involved one's whole life. Truth could not be attained by reason; it required a leap of faith, and faith was a gift from God.

This was particularly true in the case of Christianity, Kierkegaard believed. The idea of Jesus being both God and human seemed to contradict itself because God was wholly and infinitely different from humanity. That Jesus was both God and man was a divine truth, which could not be understood by human reason. Belief in the divinity of Jesus required the gift of faith and called for total and unquestioning obedience to God. Kierkegaard said that no trust could be placed in human systems of any sort—be they philosophical, doctrinal, scientific, or ecclesiastical. Indeed Kierkegaard maintained that the Christianity of the New Testament was nowhere to be found in official churches. He attacked the Lutheran Church of Denmark for failing to preserve the "scandal" of true Christianity, for replacing it with lukewarm formulas and practices.

Kierkegaard attracted attention in his own country during his lifetime, but he was little known outside it when he died in 1855. Only in the twentieth century did his thought be-

gin to exert a strong influence on both religious and secular thinkers, including Karl Barth, Martin Heidegger, Jean Paul Sartre, and Albert Camus.

4. During the 1800s several Roman Catholics reported visions of the Virgin Mary. One of the most famous and moving of these was a series of visions to Bernadette Soubirous in Lourdes, France. Lourdes became a place of pilgrimage.

During the nineteenth century a number of Roman Catholics reported that the Virgin Mary had appeared to them. In 1830 Catherine Labouré had visions of the Virgin in Paris. In 1846 two young shepherds reported visions of her at La Salette, France. But the series of visions which would have the greatest influence were those reported in 1858 by a poor young girl named Bernadette Soubirous.

Bernadette lived in the small village of Lourdes, France, at the foot of the Pyrenées, near Spain. On February 11, 1858, she and two other girls went out to gather wood at a nearby stream. Lagging behind the others, Bernadette suddenly saw a beautiful lady smiling at her from a grotto in an area known as Massabielle. During the next few weeks the lady appeared to Bernadette a number of times. Reports of the apparitions spread, some cures took place, and large crowds gath-

ered at the grotto each day to watch Bernadette as she knelt and prayed the rosary with the lady. The watchers could not see the lady, but they were deeply impressed by Bernadette's devout, prayerful manner.

Bernadette's parents and parish priest were greatly disturbed, but Bernadette herself remained calm and answered questions in a frank, simple way.

At first the lady did not say who she was, though Bernadette asked her again and again. At last the lady said, "I am the Immaculate Conception."

The dogma of the Immaculate Conception of Mary had been proclaimed four years earlier, and Bernadette may have heard the phrase in church or school, but it is doubtful that she understood its meaning. But when she repeated the lady's name to adults, they realized that the lady was saying that she was Mary, the mother of Jesus.

The lady gave Bernadette messages for the people: They were to do penance and pray for the conversion of sinners, and a chapel was to be built at Massabielle.

Fourteen years later, after a long and thorough examination, authorities of the Roman Catholic Church formally recognized that the apparitions of Mary to Bernadette were authentic. Bernadette was then in a convent, where she led a life of prayer, service, and penance until her death in 1879. Lourdes became a place of pilgrimage, and it still draws many people today.

5. The papacy of Pius IX lasted for thirty-two years—the longest of any pope. Some of his actions, such as publishing his Syllabus of Errors (1864), brought criticism from both Catholic and other Christian Churches. In 1870 he called the First Vatican Council, which proclaimed the dogma of papal infallibility.

Pope Pius IX reigned as pope for thirty-two years (1846-1878), longer than any other pope in church history. Some of his actions after returning to Rome in 1850 led to bitter criticism in his own day, even from Roman Catholics. He tried to set forth the position of the Church on various issues in a clearcut way, but it seems that he did not distinguish clearly between those people directly attacking the rights of the Church and others whose views concerned political and social issues mainly. Shortly before his death he himself admitted that much had changed in the world, that his policies belonged to a bygone day.

One example of Pius IX's approach and the problems it raised is the Syllabus of Errors he attached to an encyclical (papal letter) published in 1864. (A syllabus is a collection or list.) In the Syllabus, Pius IX collected eighty statements on a wide variety of subjects taken from his own earlier writings. Unfortunately, when the statements were taken out of their original documents, their real meaning was often hard to understand.

Some of the errors listed by the Pope dealt with religious doctrine, such as the existence of God and the divinity of Christ. Other errors dealt with certain modern ideas. One statement said that it was error to expect the pope to go along with liberalism and progress.

Naturally, some people, especially those who had liberal ideas, were irritated by this papal list. Apparently the pope and his advisers had not stopped to think of the effect of the Syllabus on people of good will.

The furor raised by the Syllabus was partially silenced by a pamphlet written by a liberal French bishop, Felix Dupanloup. He explained that the pope was speaking of an ideal world, but that the demands of the real world made it necessary to tolerate liberal ideals and institutions. Pope Pius IX accepted this interpretation.

In 1869 Pius IX summoned an ecumenical council, called the First Vatican Council. Because war broke out between France and Prussia in 1870, the council sessions stopped, and it never completed its work. Before dissolving, the council had drawn up a constitution which rejected certain errors and reaffirmed the supernatural character of Christian revelation. And it formally affirmed the universal spiritual jurisdiction of the pope in the Roman Catholic Church and also his infallibility. Saying that the pope was infallible meant that he could not make a mistake when he defined doctrines concerning faith and morals in an official, authoritative way as the supreme authority in the Church.

In May and June of 1870 there were long debates about the doctrine of infallibility. More than a few bishops clearly felt that it would be unwise to proclaim such a doctrine, even though it might be true. Some bishops, about one-eighth of the total, left the council in order to avoid voting on infallibility, which was approved by the vast majority of remaining bishops. Within a short time all the bishops, even those very few who had had doubts of its truth, accepted the doctrine of infallibility.

6. The movement known as nationalism began to grow in the 1800s. Nationalism was based on the belief that people with the same language, culture, history, and traditions should form their own nation-state, instead of being ruled by a foreign power. The Germanic, Italian, and Greek peoples and the Balkan countries began to seek independence as nations. Later, deep loyalty to one's own nation and support for its growth became a widespread and long-lasting attitude.

The Romantic movement of the early nineteenth century noted the importance of differences in language, history, tradition, and culture among the various peoples of Europe. Many Europeans felt that each people should have an opportunity to develop its own distinctive way of life. This attitude gave a strong push to the movement known as nationalism. Many different people sought to create their own nation-state—a self-governing region inhabited by people who spoke the same language and shared the same cultural background.

But the political makeup of Europe was the result of history, and it seemed to show little respect for the principles of nationalism. For example, Great Britain ruled Ireland even though most Irish people were Roman Catholic and did not want union with Great Britain. The Hapsburg Empire took in Austria, parts of Italy, parts of Poland, and much of Hungary and Bohemia. Italians, Slavs, and Hungarians yearned for greater freedom and control over their own lives.

Italian-speaking and German-speaking areas were at least united by language and culture, even though these areas were not independent, united nations. The German-speaking world was made up of many different states. Austria and Prussia were competing to become the dominant German region, and there were different ideas about how German-speaking areas might be organized into a larger unity. Much of Italy, too, was controlled by Austria, though some sections of Italy were independent. The European area which seemed closest to the nineteenth-century ideal of a nation-state

was France, where Napoleon III had proclaimed the Second Empire in 1852.

There were growing political tensions within each political area. Peoples in multicultural groupings, such as those within the Hapsburg Empire, began to push for greater political independence. In more culturally unified areas, such as France, rulers still faced the problems of turning political unity into national unity. Regional divisions had to be overcome. Economic life, education, and government administration had to be organized and carried out in a more truly national way.

There was also much competition among states and nations. As the century went on, states tried to get more territory for themselves, often at the expense of other states. There were regional conflicts in such places as Belgium, the Palatinate, Luxembourg, and areas of central Germany. Austria and France had territorial designs on Italy. Greece had won independence from the Ottoman Empire in 1830. The Balkan countries also wanted more independence and this led to a weakening of Turkish power.

The new political forces in Europe and the influence of nationalism posed problems for the Roman Catholic Church. Even in largely Catholic nations such as France there were efforts to downplay the role of the pope, since it implied allegiance to an authority outside the boundaries of the nation. There were also efforts to create national churches fairly free of papal rule. Church life in a nation, many officials thought, should fit in with the needs and practices of the government.

7. In Europe in the mid 1800s arguments raged about separating the power of the State from the authority of the Church. Traditional European practice was that the State supported an established Church. In the United States, however, there was no established Church.

For many centuries in various European countries, the Church had some legal authority over people's lives. But in the nineteenth century, many governments wanted to take away or at least reduce the Church's legal power to control certain actions of citizens. Conflict between Church and State came largely on matters of education and marriage. Some other problems arose over public displays of religion, such as processions and wearing clerical clothes in public; the tax-exempt status of churches was also opposed by some citizens and officials.

There was a movement to separate the Church and the State so that they would operate independently of each other. This issue caused much bitterness in both Protestant and Catholic regions. In the mid 1800s, many

members of the larger denominations (Catholics, Lutherans, Calvinists, Anglicans) believed that religion was a public rather than a private matter and that Christian nations should replace the medieval ideal of a united Christendom.

As liberal and nationalist views gained more influence in Europe, members of parliaments might be conservatives, moderates, republicans, or even socialists. Efforts were made to restrict the Church's role in such areas as education and politics. Church members wondered whether they should join an existing political party or create their own. Some accepted the new situation with more or less enthusiasm. Others felt that they should take part in the new setup and bring Christian influences to government and society.

The situation of the Christian churches in the United States was very different. In this new nation, all faiths were "starting even," something that could not happen in the old countries of Europe. American Catholic bishops supported the Constitution, which guaranteed freedom of religion, and they wanted the Church and State to be separate.

8. In 1870 Italy was unified after a revolutionary war. Victor Emmanuel II became king and the Church lost the Papal States. In protest at this armed conquest, Pope Pius IX retreated to the Vatican Palace and refused to have anything to do with the new Italian government.

In 1852, Count Camillo di Cavour, premier of Sardinia, began a drive to unify Italy. Though premier of the island of Sardinia, Cavour lived in Turin, in northern Italy. Backed by support from France and England and by local forces in various parts of Italy, Cavour managed to take over almost all the area in the Italian peninsula. The age-old papal territory was gradually reduced to Rome and its suburbs. In 1870 the city of Rome was conquered, and the next year Rome became the capital of the new kingdom of Italy.

King Victor Emmanuel II was the ruler, and he took over the papal palace called the Quirinal. Pius IX retreated to the Vatican Palace. The Italian government offered to pay the pope a sum of money each year, but Pope Pius IX refused to have any dealings with the new government on the grounds that he was the victim of aggression.

In 1874 Pius IX issued a statement forbidding Roman Catholics in Italy to participate in the political life of the nation. Catholics, however, were active in journalism and social work. Many papers and magazines under the editorial direction of priests were established. The Italian Catholic Youth Organization was founded in 1868, and Catholic clubs grew among university students.

Relations between the papacy and the Italian government were established under Pius XI in 1929, under an agreement with Benito Mussolini, the head of the Italian government.

9. During the years of turmoil in Italy in the 1800s, John Bosco began his mission of caring for and educating poor, homeless boys. He began this work as a youth, attracting boys with his show of magic tricks and juggling, which he followed with a homily on the gospels. John Bosco formed a new community of priests called Salesians, who continue his mission.

Religious orders took a major part in the social and charitable work of the Roman Catholic Church during the nineteenth century. They continued to grow in numbers and importance. One such new group was the Oratory of St. Francis de Sales, whose members are also known as the Salesian Fathers. The Oratory was founded in 1859 in Turin by John Bosco.

John Bosco (1815–1888) came from a poor peasant family, and his father died when John was two. John knew what being poor meant, but he had little idea of the problems caused by poverty in cities until he entered the seminary to study for the priesthood. During his training he found time to visit prisons and make friends with young delinquents and criminals. He gathered them on Sundays for meetings where they prayed, learned about religion, and played. John had a knack for winning their friendship. On the advice of his priestly counselor, who was a prison chaplain for criminals on death row, John Bosco decided to devote himself to young people who were on the verge of getting into serious trouble.

He attracted crowds of youngsters by putting on a show of magic tricks and juggling acts. After the show, he spoke to them about the gospel message. He did not hesitate to go hunting for them in the streets or in their favorite hangouts. He purchased a small house in Turin, which was the start of the Oratory of St. Francis de Sales. It provided homeless boys with a place to live, and it soon expanded into much more than that. There the boys got schooling, learned trades, and found the support and loving guidance of people interested in them. Other men joined John in his work to form a new community of priests, who came to be known as the Salesian Fathers. Eventually the Oratory also had a printing shop, and John Bosco founded a school for girls with the help of Mary Mazzarello.

Some civil authorities were more than a little suspicious of the Oratory. What exactly was this priest doing with all those juvenile delinquents and "hoods"? In fact, he was changing the course of many young lives by teaching the youngsters a useful trade and feeding them needed doses of respect and love. He appealed to their good side, and many responded. By the time John Bosco died, his center in Turin was training over seven hundred boys, and his work had spread to other countries.

10. Jean Dunant, a Swiss Calvinist, experienced the horrors of brutal war and wanted to help the wounded. He founded the Red Cross in 1864, and the organization spread throughout the world. Today the Red Cross also helps victims of such disasters as earthquakes and floods.

Solferino was a small town in northern Italy. There, on June 24, 1859, French and Sardinian troops fought against Austrian forces in the course of the war for Italian independence. Emperor Napoleon III ruled France at the time, and Emperor Francis Joseph ruled the Austrian Empire. The battle was very bloody and cost many lives. Even the rulers were shocked by the heavy losses and the terrible cost of the battle. There were 18,000 killed and wounded on the French-Sardinian side, which won the battle. Austrian losses were about 20,000. Many of the wounded were in terrible condition. Newly built railroads had gotten troops to the battle zone fairly quickly, but there was a desperate lack of food, water, medicine, and doctors.

The sight of the awful massacre left a deep impression on one man who taken part in the battle: Jean Henri Dunant (1828–1910). Dunant, who lived in Geneva, was a Swiss Calvinist of liberal and social-minded views. He wanted to something to make war less

brutal and to aid its victims. His idea attracted attention when he wrote an account of the battle at Solferino, *Un souvenir de Solferino* (*A Remembrance of Solferino*), which was published in 1862. Home again, Dunant began to urge the Swiss to establish an organization to aid those victimized by war. The idea was favorably received, and in 1864 an international conference was called. It drew up the first Geneva Convention, the aim of which was to "better the condition of the wounded and sick of armies in the field." Twelve of the nations represented at the conference signed the document. The medical staffs of armies were to be considered neutral, the sick and wounded were to be treated humanely, and civilians were to be given decent protection. It was decided to make up an international emblem or badge to mark people and supplies connected with the new movement. In honor of Dunant, the emblem chosen was the Swiss flag with colors reversed: a red cross on a white background.

Member associations of the Red Cross soon arose in many countries. In 1867 the International Red Cross Conference was formed as the chief governing body of the organization. In later years, further changes and additions were made to the Geneva Convention. The Red Cross soon was performing outstanding work in war and other situations of disaster, such as floods and earthquakes. For example, it came to the aid of victims of the 1906 earthquake in San Francisco and the 1908 earthquake in Messina (Italy). Its work in war and peace has made it one of the best-known organizations in the world, and people of many different backgrounds and beliefs have participated in its work.

Dunant participated in other causes and wrote several books. He shared the first Nobel Peace Prize in 1901 with Frederick Passy (1822–1912), a French economist who dedicated his energies to the promotion of international peace.

11. Near the end of the 1800s, France moved toward separation of Church and State. Liberals often attacked the Church, and conservatives supported it. During this same time, though, religious life and practice revived in France.

During the reign of Emperor Napoleon III (1852–1870), the Roman Catholic Church was able to carry on its work in France without too much difficulty. The moral and material conditions of the clergy improved, the number of ordinations increased, and religious congregations grew. Many nuns took part in charitable and educational work. Catholic schools were put on an equal footing with public schools.

After France's defeat by Prussia in 1871, Parisians of many different political opinions rejected the existing national government and set up a regime for the city called the commune of Paris. Extreme views soon took over, and hostages were shot—including the archbishop of Paris. The French national government attacked Paris and won the city. More than 17,000 people (including women and children) were executed. Memories of all this created bitter political relations between French liberals and conservatives.

In the following decades, religious life and practice revived in France. But Catholics were often thought to be looking for the return of the monarchy and the end of newly-won freedoms. Many French people stopped practicing Roman Catholicism, and there were riots and disorders during church processions. Workmen felt little loyalty to the Church. Rationalism, positivism, and anti-church Freemasonry appealed to many people. When liberal factions could, they passed laws hostile to the Church. The French clergy, in turn, was basically hostile to the new republic.

In the 1880s, the republican government of France began moving toward final and complete separation of Church and State. The separation was enacted in 1905, having been somewhat hastened by the actions of French Catholics in what is known as "the Dreyfus affair."

Captain Alfred Dreyfus was a French Jew unjustly accused of being a spy for the Germans. Though he insisted that he was innocent, he was condemned to life imprisonment on Devil's Island in Guiana.

A few years later, evidence was found that Captain Dreyfus had been tried unjustly and that another officer was guilty. Many people wanted Dreyfus brought to France for a new trial, but many others objected. They disliked Dreyfus because he was a Jew and because he supported the republican government. To many French Catholics, opposing Dreyfus became a symbolic way of showing their loyalty to the Church and their opposition to the government. Dreyfus was eventually freed, and the anti-semitism and bigotry of many French Catholics brought severe criticism of the Church.

12. Prussia, the leading state in the North German Confederation, proclaimed William I emperor of Germany in 1870. The Catholic minority in the new empire formed the Central Party to represent its interests.

Efforts to reunite German-speaking areas grew during the nineteenth century. The empire of Austria and the kingdom of Prussia wished to lead and dominate this effort, but Prussia won out. Led by the able and remarkable Chancellor Otto von Bismarck, Prussia gradually increased its territory and won over German-speaking allies. In 1866 Prussia went to war with Austria and defeated the latter's armies thoroughly and quickly. Then Prussia and its North German Confederation, under Bismarck's shrewd direction, defeated France in 1871. William I of Prussia was proclaimed emperor of Germany. The new German Empire was a confederation of principalities including Prussia, Baden, Bavaria, and others.

Roman Catholics were a minority in the new Germany. There was suspicion of the Catholic Church and even outright hostility among many officials in Prussia. The Prussian constitution of 1850 was far less liberal than that of other states in the federation, and Bismarck himself saw danger from Roman Catholicism in several ways.

The Catholic Center Party, formed in 1870, seemed a threat to Protestant interests, as did the existence of large numbers of Catholics in some of the member states such as Bavaria. Bismarck wanted to increase the central power of the new German nation, and he saw Catholic loyalty to Rome as an opposing force. The proclamation of papal infallibility by Vatican I in 1870 also helped to feed Bismarck's anti-Catholic Church sentiments, and he felt that actions taken against the Catholic Church would find favor with liberal factions in Germany.

The Austrian empire faced discontent and desire for independence among its member nations.

Vienna

Budapest

The unequal treatment of its member nations was a great weakness in the Austrian empire, which was strong in many other ways. Austria was a multilingual (many languages) empire and included Bohemians, Hungarians, Slovaks, and Italians, dominated by the German-speaking Austrians.

Defeats by the Prussians and Italians indicated that reforms were necessary to hold the sections of the empire together. In 1867 Hungary was given equal footing with Austria, and the Hapsburg emperor became chief executive of both countries. Each section had its own parliament and administration, though foreign policy and military and financial affairs were to be handled in common.

While this agreement soothed the Hungarians, it gave no real recognition to the national yearnings of the Italian and Slavic groups in the empire. In Croatia, for example, Bishop Strossmayer was a very active spokesman for the national and religious interests of the Croatians. Faithful to the Hapsburg monarchy, he opposed excessive political centralization. Faithful to the Catholic Church, he opposed excessive church centralization in Rome. He was one of the last bishops to send his written assent to the proclamation of papal infallibility.

Friedrich Dani...t Schleiermacher
1768-1834

13. Protestant theologians
and scholars published
important works
during this era. Among
them were Tholuck, Strauss,
Schleiermacher, Ritschl,
Troeltsch, and von Harnack.

The study of theology and Christian thought has always been nurtured and encouraged by most Protestant churches. During the nineteenth century, a whole series of scholars and thinkers set to work in German-speaking lands. The philosophy of Hegel had great influence on their work.

The outstanding theologian in the earlier part of the 1800s was Friedrich Schleiermacher, who stressed the importance of religion in the intellectual and cultural life of humanity. (This was discussed in chapter 44 of *The Church in Revolutionary Times*.)

Friederich Tholuck (1799–1877), a disciple of Schleiermacher, lived and taught in Berlin. He was not the profound theologian that Schleiermacher was, but he had a deep influence on many people through his sermons and his pastoral work among students. Tholuck sought to give deeper meaning to the religious movement known as the Awakening, stressing a return to the central teachings of the New Testament and Luther's proclamation of these teachings.

David F. Strauss (1808–1874) was a follower of Hegel. He created a sensation with his *Life of Jesus* (1835). Accepting the historical reality of Jesus, he declared that the gospel accounts were unreliable legends or "myths" akin to earlier models in the Old Testament.

Albrecht Ritschl (1822–1889) was a leading theologian in the latter half of the nineteenth century. He stirred up new interest in church history, biblical study, dogmatic theology (the study of church dogmas), and practical or pastoral theology (applying the Church's teachings). Ritschl stressed the importance of the Church, the Bible, and Luther. At the same time, he denied the doctrine of original sin and emphasized the potential goodness and progress open to human beings. His chief work was the *Christian Doctrine of Justification and Reconciliation* (1870–1874).

Adolf von Harnack (1851–1930) published his great work on the *History of Dogma* between 1886 and 1890. He sought to show that the simple spiritual and ethical religion of Jesus had been distorted and buried under later dogmas. The core of Christianity, von Harnack said, was a simple and enlightened moral code of behavior, perfectly suited to the modern world.

Ernst Troeltsch (1865–1923) was deeply impressed by the growth of the historical sciences. He came to feel that religion was deeply influenced by the surrounding society and culture, just as society and culture were influenced by religion. His work on the *Social Teachings of the Christian Churches* (1912) remains important even today.

14. Bishop von Ketteler of Mainz, Germany, took the lead in Catholic social action. He shared the hard life of his peasants and realized that the Church should support their demands for justice. By his books and actions he provided a program for improving conditions for workers. During this same time, von Wichern, a Protestant preacher, worked in Hamburg to better the living conditions of the laboring class.

Industrial development began somewhat later in Germany than in other Western nations, but the Catholic social movement began soon after the onset of industrialization. German Catholics interested in the social question made real efforts to protect workers from uncontrolled exploitation by the wealthy. Self-employed laborers and peasants were the first to be defended and supported, but gradually the growing question of factory work attracted attention.

An important role in all this was played by the dynamic Bishop William von Ketteler of Mainz. He had served as a priest in a poor rural parish in Hanover. There he shared the hard life of the peasants, lived with them during a terrible famine, and tried to take care of them during a typhoid epidemic. Reflecting on their living conditions, he came to see the needs of the poor working classes and

to lend church support to their demands for greater justice.

In 1848 Ketteler preached a powerful series of sermons on social problems, which were later published in book form. Another book of his on *Christianity and the Labor Question* was a pioneer work in the field of Catholic social doctrine. It provided German Catholics with a program for their work.

Among other clergymen interested in helping laboring people were Adolf Kölping and Johann von Wichern. Kölping, a Catholic priest of the Rhineland, founded a Journeyman's Union. In Hamburg, von Wichern, a Protestant preacher, did fine work in training lay people to care for the needy. In 1849 he published a book which vividly described the living conditions of poor workers in various German cities.

15. At the end of the 1800s, Spain had become a small, weak nation. Traditional ways of acting and thinking clashed with modern ideas. Many liberals were against the Church because it would not give its large tracts of land to the farmers of Spain.

In the mid 1800s Spain faced many problems. Some regions were economically well off because they had benefited from economic development and from trade with the Spanish colonies in the Americas. Other regions were poor and saw no hope of bettering conditions. And most of the Spanish colonies had been lost in the early 1800s.

Spanish liberals called for modernizing the country, and this often included breaking up the large landholdings of the Roman Catholic Church and of the aristocratic families and giving the land to small farmers. Usually the Church and the old families opposed this idea. As a result, liberals were often anti-Church.

In 1833, a long crisis began when Ferdinand VII died and left the crown to his three-year-old daughter, Isabella II. Don Carlos, the king's brother, claimed the crown for himself, and many Spaniards supported his claim. Queen Isabella's reign was very stormy, and in 1868 she was dethroned by a revolution and had to leave Spain. Seven years of political unrest and civil war followed. In 1875 Isabella's son was brought back to Spain to become King Alfonso XII, and a year later Spain adopted a constitution modeled somewhat on the British form of government.

In the following years trade unions gained more power, and the government was some-times controlled by liberals, sometimes by conservatives. Anti-Church feelings were strong among liberals, and conflicts between Church and State grew bitter in the late 1800s. Catholics were also divided among themselves. Some dreamed of returning to the olden times; others felt it was more realistic to try to work peacefully with the liberals.

In 1898 Spain was defeated in a war with the United States and lost the last of its colonies in the New World. This defeat greatly shocked Spaniards, especially the younger generation of writers and thinkers. They pondered the tragic destiny of Spain, once a mighty empire but now a small, weak nation.

16. A period of growth and progress for the Catholic Church was under way in Great Britain. The Catholic Emancipation Act in 1829 had removed laws against Catholics, and in 1850 the Roman Catholic hierarchy was restored in England and Wales. The situation of the Church in Ireland was also improving.

Around the middle of the nineteenth century, the Roman Catholic Church seemed to be gaining more freedom in certain Protestant sections of Europe. The Catholic Emancipation Act, removing laws against Catholics, had been passed in Great Britain in 1829. Also, the terrible famine in Ireland in 1848 made many Irish people leave their homeland (emigrate) to look for work in other countries. Many of these emigrants went to England to work in the cotton and woolen mills, and they brought their Catholic faith with them.

In 1850 Pius IX restored the Catholic hierarchy (system of church government) in England and Wales. Nicholas Cardinal Wiseman became archbishop of Westminster, and twelve other bishops were created. There was strong Protestant reaction against having Roman Catholic bishops in England, but Cardinal Wiseman did a good job of calming Protestant fears and starting the reorganization of the Catholic Church. Encouraged, Pius IX restored the Catholic hierarchy in Calvinistic Holland in 1853, and the Catholic Church was soon making progress there.

In Ireland the situation of the Catholic Church was improving, but nationalism and the issue of land ownership were becoming very important. The Irish wanted more voice in their government, and they wanted to reclaim their lands, many of which were now owned by English landowners. These influences gradually drew the largely Catholic population of the country toward greater militancy. Many bishops opposed the trend, but many priests sympathized with the people among whom they lived. The fight to win freedom from England was called the Fenian movement after a legendary band of ancient Irish warriors. The Fenian movement continued throughout the latter half of the nineteenth century despite arrests and executions. A former Fenian, Arthur Griffith, went on to organize the Sinn Fein movement around the turn of the twentieth century.

In 1879 an Anglo-Irish Protestant named Charles Stewart Parnell began attracting Irish Catholics to his Nationalist Party. Soon four-fifths of the Irish members of the British parliament were of his party. They demanded a separate Irish parliament and Irish Home Rule. (Home Rule meant that the Irish would have control over their own internal affairs.) Agitation in Ireland and in the British parliament failed to win Home Rule from the British parliament. When World War I started in 1914, Ireland was still ruled by England.

17. A number of reformers were active in the field of social service in the 1800s. Among them was Elizabeth Fry, who worked to improve living conditions in prisons in England. In the United States, Louis Dwight, Dorothea Dix, and William and Catherine Booth carried out important missions among unfortunate people.

During the 1800s people of different religious beliefs and even no religious beliefs worked to help victims of poverty, mistreatment, and neglect. They did not wait for government or church institutions to back them up.

One such pioneer figure in England was Elizabeth Fry (1780–1845), a Quaker. Elizabeth was deeply religious and even led religious services. But her great work was prison reform, which she began in 1813 to improve conditions for women in Newgate prison. Besides trying to deal with prisoners as human beings, Elizabeth wanted males and females to have separate quarters in prisons, to be given worthwhile employment, and to be provided with religious instruction and education. Her work at Newgate impressed government officials, and her methods were tried in other prisons. She traveled to Europe to inspect prisons, and she also opened up soup kitchens in London for the poor and hungry.

Similar reform campaigns were seen on a wide front in the United States before the Civil War. Work for prison reform was carried on by the Reverend Louis Dwight, for example. He urged the use of cell blocks and group labor instead of solitary confinement and solitary labor. First tried at the prison in Auburn, New York, this came to be known as the Auburn System and was copied elsewhere in the country.

A truly remarkable reformer was Dorothea Dix (1802–1887). Inspired by the Reverend William Ellery Channing, whose words and example influenced many Americans in the first half of the nineteenth century, Dorothea set out to improve the terrible situation of the mentally ill. In her day these sick people were often placed in prisons alongside criminals, even though they had committed no crime. In 1842 she wrote a famous memorandum to the legislature of the state of Massachusetts, and in the following year efforts

were begun to improve hospital care of the mentally ill. Hospitals for them began to arise in many states, and Dorothea's work influenced Canada and Europe as well.

The start of another important Christian social organization was due to an English husband and wife. William Booth was a Methodist minister who began to work on his own in 1861. Greatly helped by his wife Catherine, he went to London and began a revival society (a society to revive religious feeling). In 1878 the organization got its current name: the Salvation Army. Two years later it began a branch in the United States. Its members were to lead lives of great purity and religious seriousness, and their concern for every aspect of human life led them into an astonishing range of activities and services all over the world.

18. John Henry Newman, leader of the Oxford Movement in the Church of England, became a Roman Catholic in 1845. He introduced the Oratory of Philip Neri into England and founded one oratory in London, one in Birmingham. Newman wrote important literary and theological works, including *Grammar of Assent,* in which he showed how conscience provides a sure path to the knowledge of God.

John Henry Newman (1801–1890), whom we met in the previous volume as leader of the Oxford Movement, went to Rome shortly after his conversion to Catholicism and was ordained a priest there. He became devoted to the sixteenth-century St. Philip Neri and decided to introduce St. Philip's institute of priests, the Oratorians, into England. This he did in 1849, founding one Oratory in Birmingham and another in London.

Newman himself lived and worked in Birmingham, where he and his fellow Oratorians staffed a parish and a school for boys. He continued to write books and deliver lectures and sermons which gained him nationwide attention. One of his most beautiful sermons was titled "The Second Spring"; it expressed the hopes that Roman Catholics had in the 1850s that their church would flourish again in England as it had before the Reformation. He wrote novels and poetry as well, and his long poem, *The Dream of Gerontius* (1865),

which depicted the soul's journey to God at the moment of death, was later set to music by the famous composer Sir Edward Elgar.

But Newman's most important works were his theological ones. Among these was his "Letter to the Duke of Norfolk" which defended Catholics against the charge that they could not be good citizens because of their loyalty to the pope. In *Grammar of Assent* he showed how human conscience provided a sure path to the knowledge of God.

Newman endured many failures and frustrations during his life as a Catholic. The Irish bishops asked him to found and head a Catholic University in Dublin, but after years of work on Newman's part the project came to nothing. The English bishops wanted him to prepare a new English translation of the Bible, but then, for reasons Newman was never told, they dropped the idea. Some of Newman's fellow converts to Catholicism spread the story that he was not really a wholehearted Catholic, and at least a few high officials in Rome belived it. This hurt Newman deeply, because he was totally dedicated to the Catholic Church, which he had given up much to join.

So he was glad when in 1864, an Anglican clergyman in a magazine article, questioned Newman's sincerity and truthfulness. This insult gave him the chance to defend himself by telling the story of his life as an Anglican and of his reasons for becoming a Catholic. He called this book *Apologia pro Vita Sua (Defense of My Life)*. It was received with enthusiasm by Anglicans and Catholics alike and has been recognized ever since as one of the greatest spiritual autobiographies ever written.

Newman continued to his last days—he died in 1890, at the age of 89—to serve all Christian believers with his writings in behalf of the faith. He finally received some signs of recognition for his efforts. In 1877 he was appointed an honorary member of the Anglican College at Oxford, which he had attended as a young man. Two years later Pope Leo XIII named him a cardinal. When he heard of this honor Newman said, "The cloud is lifted from me forever."

19. Henry Edward Manning had been a friend and co-worker of Newman's in the Oxford Movement. In 1851 he, too, became a Roman Catholic. Eventually Manning became a cardinal and a leader of Roman Catholics in England. He supported the rights of working people and improved the education of the poor.

Great men do not always get along with each other. A good example of this fact was the relationship between Cardinal Newman and Henry Edward Manning (1808–1872), who also was a cardinal of the Roman Catholic Church.

Both of them had been Anglican clergymen, both had been educated at Oxford, and, though Manning was six years younger than Newman, they were friends and co-workers in the Oxford Movement. When Newman became a Catholic (1845), Manning remained in the Church of England. He was eloquent and hardworking, and everybody predicted that he would rise to the highest office that that Church had to offer. But then, in 1851, because he was convinced that the Church of England taught false doctrine about the sacrament of Baptism, he too became a Catholic.

Because Manning's wife had died years before, it was possible for him to be ordained in the celibate priesthood of the Catholic Church. He quickly became a leader of the Catholic community in England, and in 1865 he was named Archbishop of Westminster. He proved to be a very efficient and sometimes stern ruler. He was also strict and narrow in his ideas and was often impatient with other Catholics who did not agree with him on one matter or another. He was especially impatient with Newman, who, he thought, was not enthusiastic enough in supporting certain ideas. For instance, Newman believed in the doctrine of papal infallibility, but he thought it should not be defined at Vatican Council I, because the definition might lead many non-Catholics to despise the Church. Manning, on the contrary, was a leading champion of the definition.

Over this and similar differences their friendship ended. The basic reason probably was that while Newman was a thinker who saw how complicated religious questions could be, Manning was a practical man who saw these issues in simple terms and above all wanted to get things done. And it was in getting things done that Manning proved to be, in his own way, a great churchman and accomplished what Newman could never have accomplished.

Manning set out to build a network of Catholic schools and to improve the education of the poor. He was prominent in social work of all kinds. He strongly supported the rights of working people who were often exploited by low wages and terrible conditions in the factories and mines. He interceded with Prime Minister Gladstone, who had been his closest friend when they were students together at Oxford, in behalf of the poor Irish peasants who were being driven from their land. There is no doubt that Manning's social action in England contributed to Leo XIII's great encyclical on the social question, *Rerum novarum,* which we will discuss in later chapters.

In 1889 the very badly paid dock workers of London called a strike. They trusted Cardinal Manning more than any other public person, and they appealed to him for help. He responded by taking the lead in their successful negotiations with management. The aged Newman sent him a warm note of congratulations. Three years later, when Manning died, hundreds of thousands of ordinary people paid tribute to him by lining the route of his funeral procession.

20. The question of slavery in the United States led to a bloody civil war (1860–1864). After the war, Methodists, Baptists, and Presbyterians had Southern branches. Also, the Black Christian churches now began to become a major factor in the American religious scene. The Roman Catholic Church grew larger, fed by the waves of Catholic immigrants. Some problems arose because German immigrants held on to their culture and language and were suspicious of the Irish clergy and bishops.

During the first half of the 1800s, more states were added to the United States. Some states allowed slavery and some did not, and the debate about slavery grew stronger and more bitter. By the 1850s, the opposing viewpoints were rapidly hardening into fierce beliefs. In 1860–1861, eleven Southern states, insisting that they had the right as sovereign states to maintain slavery, withdrew from the federal union and formed the Confederate States. The other states would not agree to this, and the result was a bloody civil war between North and South which lasted four years.

Many Christian churches were divided along sectional lines during the war. Even in churches which did not divide openly, many members went along with the views of their home region. Christian chaplains went to comfort and aid the warring soldiers in both camps.

When the Civil War was over, sectional differences remained among the reunited states. The Episcopal and the Roman Catholic churches each remained united under its own head, but some other churches now had Southern branches. For example, there were now Southern Baptists, Methodists, and Presbyterians. Black members were transferred to separate churches of their own. This led to an important development in American church history: the rise of Black Christian churches. While some had been in existence before the Civil War, these Black Christian churches now began to grow into a major factor on the American religious scene. For example, by 1896 the African Methodist Episcopal Church claimed more than 450,000

members. These churches were an important influence on the lives of many Black people during the years following the Civil War and on into the twentieth century when Black people were deprived of their civil and human rights.

As Americans continued to move westward, they pushed back the native Indians and repeatedly violated treaties with them. Reformers spoke out for the neglected rights of the Indians, and many churches tried to help. But the underlying ideal was to convert the Indians to both the religion and the culture of the White Christian. Today Indians are actively claiming their rights under the Constitution, including rights guaranteed in legal treaties of the past.

The Catholic Church continued to grow after the Civil War, nourished by wave after wave of immigrants. German Catholics became the most numerous group in some dioceses, and they held on to their German language and culture. Serious disagreements arose because they felt that they were not properly represented in the American hierarchy, which was largely of Irish descent. The more relaxed attitude of the hierarchy towards Church-State relations also seemed suspicious to some German laypeople, clergy, and religious. But the American Church held together as it proceeded to tackle the problems posed by immigration, giant industrialism, labor conditions, and recurring anti-Catholic attacks.

21. Leo XIII became pope in 1878, and a new era began for the papacy. Leo XIII strongly emphasized the values in earlier Catholic tradition, but he was also open to dealing with the modern world and its problems.

When a papal conclave met in February 1878 to elect a new pope after the death of Pius IX, much had changed. The papacy no longer owned any papal states, and the Vatican seemed to be an uncertain shelter in Rome, the capital of a recently independent Italy. Indeed there had been suggestions that the papal election be held outside Italy.

The task of preparing the conclave fell to Cardinal Gioacchino Pecci of Perugia. He handled his task calmly and well, convinced that the conclave should be held in Rome. He already had a fine reputation for his work in Perugia, and he was elected pope on February 20, 1878. He took the name Leo XIII.

Pecci came from central Italy of a noble family. Born in 1810, he chose quite early in life to become a priest. A brilliant student, he attracted the attention of the papal advisers

and carried out several important assignments for the Church. At the age of only thirty-six he became archbishop of Perugia. He organized schools and charitable works and showed concern for the education and spiritual development of his priests. He was much more open than Pius IX. His general attitude was one of openness to new ideas and new advancements in scholarship and science, though he held firmly to traditional church doctrines and teachings.

Leo XIII set a new tone in the Catholic Church's approach to the modern world. Two of his earliest encyclicals (letters) were *Aeterni Patris* (1879) and *Immortale Dei* (1885). (Encyclicals are written in Latin and take their names from the opening words.) In the first encyclical Leo XIII presented Thomas Aquinas as the great scholarly model for

Catholic thinking. The philosophy of Aquinas was to be the official philosophy of the Church, and its study was to be required. Thomas, after all, had tried to confront the new thinking of his own day and relate it to the traditional teachings of the Church. In *Immortale Dei* Leo XIII outlined how Catholics could act as good, responsible citizens in modern states of a more secular and democratic sort.

Almost unknown outside Italy when he was elected, and not expected to live long, Leo XIII gave new life and possibilities to the Catholic Church during his long reign of twenty-five years. It is as if this one man managed to create a whole new atmosphere for Roman Catholics to breathe, and he certainly ranks as one of the greatest popes of modern times.

22. Problems over the relationship of Church and State showed up in many countries. In sections of Germany, harsh laws were enacted against the Catholic Church, and Catholic schools were threatened. Leo XIII worked successfully to improve this situation.

As was shown in earlier chapters, liberals often were opposed to the existing status of the Catholic Church. When they gained power in government, they passed anticlerical and anti-Church measures. One very serious conflict of this sort arose in the new Germany, so that the struggle is often referred to by the German term for it: *Kulturkampf,* meaning "cultural struggle."

The aim of liberals was to eliminate the presence and influence of the Catholic Church in the school system. They planned to enact a series of laws to hinder or stop church work in schools. The German state of Baden passed such laws, but soon Prussia took the lead in a serious attack on the Catholic Church. Catholic schools were put under watch by the State, and school inspectors were to make sure that new laws were obeyed. The Jesuits were expelled from Prussia in 1872, and then from Germany as a whole. The May Laws of 1873 established rules for the training of priests and penalties for disobeying. People getting married would have to go through a civil ceremony. Candidates for church positions would have to swear an oath of loyalty to the State. There were harsh fines and prison sentences, and many churchmen went into exile.

Despite this persecution, the Catholic Center Party continued to do well in elections. By 1878 an uneasy Bismarck decided to adopt a more moderate course with Catholics. He wanted to gain Catholic support for his tariff measures, which were opposed by the liberals. Also, he needed support against rising socialist ideas and demands. The death of Pius IX and the election of Leo XIII as pope (1878) marked the start of a new situation.

On the very day of his election Leo XIII sent a letter to William I, King of Prussia and Emperor of Germany. The pope expressed hopes that better relations between Germany and the Church might be established. Gradually many German laws against the Roman Catholic Church were repealed or simply forgotten. Bishops no longer had to take an oath of loyalty to the State. Anti-Church school legislation was also dropped. Within ten years a solid working relationship had been established between Prussia and the Vatican.

23. During the second half of the nineteenth century, European workers began to gain bargaining strength. Progress was slow because they were often opposed by businessmen who had formed joint-stock companies that made them very strong. The slogan "Workers of the world, unite!" and the ideas of Karl Marx and Friedrich Engels began to spread widely.

The story of labor in the nineteenth century is a long and complicated one. Questions about working conditions and fair wages, for example, were mixed up with many other issues such as industrialization, voting rights, nationalism, liberalism, foreign competition, profits, religious ideals, and radical theories.

Certainly workers lacked political power at the start. But the owners were able to use laws, armed forces, policemen, and even hired hoodlums to defend their interests. Violence and killing were a part of the conflict between labor and business.

In England, the leader in the Industrial Revolution, some reforms and improvements for workers were won for women and children in the early part of the nineteenth century. But the major gains for workers came after 1850, when wages also rose. Still, the number of work hours per week remained high, the growing use of machinery posed dangers to health and safety, and many workers feared that machinery would take away their jobs. Workers felt, too, that owners were getting more than their fair share of the profits. At

this time businessmen were organizing joint-stock companies and large corporations, which made their position very strong. Collective organizing for businessmen came before collective bargaining for workers. But between 1864 and 1890, laws against the formation of labor unions were abolished in many countries.

"Workers of the world, unite!" The slogan and the views of Karl Marx and Friedrich Engels began to spread widely after 1850. Marx was clearly the driving genius behind the movement. The cause was "scientific" socialism which, said Marx, really explained what had been going on in history and what would happen in the future. History, he stated, was really a story of material struggle between social classes, between those who enjoyed economic, social, and political power and those who did not. Capitalism had now brought to power the middle-class owners of the means of production. But the development of capitalism would unite common workers, Marx felt, and lead them to revolt. This revolt would cause the collapse of the

capitalistic system and eventually lead to a classless society where all human beings could be equal. Religion and the State would disappear in the process.

Marx's predictions have not fared very well, but serious scholars now feel that Marx deserves to be considered as one of the major founders of modern sociology and the history of economic theories. The development of his varied views into an almost religious belief by Marxists came later.

In 1864 Marx played an important role in organizing and running the International Working Men's Association, also known as the First International. Its aim was to unite workers of many countries and give them an international outlook. The First International collapsed in 1876, and the Second International was formed in 1889. When war broke out in 1914, nationalism proved stronger than loyalty to the International, and workers joined the armies of their countries. However, Marxism became dominant in Russia following the revolution of 1917.

24. The story of a fictitious person, Stephen O'Clare, tells us about the Knights of Labor, an organization for workers in the late 1800s. The Knights were not approved by some Catholic leaders because they were a secret society. But Stephen O'Clare believed that the Knights were a good organization that would help working people.

Let us now read the story of Stephen O'Clare, an imaginary American worker of Irish background. His family had come from Ireland to Baltimore around 1828, and Stephen was born about a year later. When our story opens in 1879, Stephen is about fifty years old.

Stephen was a skilled worker who had come to Philadelphia many years earlier to work on precision naval instruments in a shipyard factory. He was liked and respected by other workers and by the managers of the business. He and his wife had six children, and one boy had become a priest. Stephen was a peaceful, easygoing man, but he was not afraid to defend himself or others when it was necessary. As a young man in Baltimore, he had joined other Roman Catholics in defending the parish church against attacks from bands of anti-Catholic Know-Nothings.

By 1879 a large number of people had come to Philadelphia to seek work. They included Irish, Italians, and Blacks from the South. Women were also employed in the factory where O'Clare worked. Skilled workers like O'Clare were not paid badly, but others did not fare so well.

One day there was a meeting of plant workers. O'Clare was upset when he heard the story of one young man who had been badly injured by a machine and could no longer work. Two Black workers also told how workers of their color tended to be treated unfairly. Several women had similar stories of unfair treatment to tell. O'Clare spoke up at the meeting, expressing anger over the conditions reported by various workers. Other workers talked about the need for organizing, and some mentioned the Knights of Labor, an organization which had been founded in 1869 by a group of Philadelphia garment workers.

The Knights of Labor had been organized as a secret organization with a complicated ritual. In 1879 its membership was still fairly small: about 10,000. O'Clare did not care too much for the idea of a secret society, which was frowned upon by the Catholic Church. But the problems of his fellow workers bothered him, and he accepted the invitation of another worker to go to an important meeting that same evening. O'Clare suspected it was a meeting of the Knights of Labor. There would be no harm in seeing what the meeting might have to do with the problems of workers.

Little did O'Clare realize that he himself would join the Knights of Labor that very evening. He found many Catholic workers there, and he liked what he heard. He was

joining an organization which grew and flourish in the first half of the 1880s, under the leadership of Terence Powderley, a Roman Catholic. At one point it had a membership of over 700,000, including some 60,000 Black workers. Then various factors worked against the organization, and other labor organizations took its place.

25. In 1887 there was danger that Pope Leo XIII would condemn the Knights of Labor because they were a secret society. Terence Powderley, leader of the Knights in the United States, dropped much of the secrecy. Also, he explained the aims of the Knights to Cardinal James Gibbons. Cardinal Gibbons then wrote to the pope and endorsed the Knights of Labor.

As time went on the Knights of Labor program and practice put them in the forefront of the labor movement. They did not favor the idea of grouping workers by crafts because they felt that modern machinery and working conditions were eliminating the old division of trades and crafts. Blacks, women, and immigrants were accepted as members. Unskilled workers as well as craftsmen could join. The Knights wanted an eight-hour work day as well as equal pay for equal work. Although their official program was against strikes, they did in fact support a series of successful local strikes between 1884 and 1886. Thousands of new members flooded into the organization.

Such attempts to organize labor met much opposition in the United States during this period. It was the Gilded Age of wealthy industrialists. Many such industrialists, and many other educated Americans, adopted a social philosophy spelled out by Herbert Spencer of England. They believed that in the business world, as in the world of nature, the fittest would survive.

There was also opposition to the Knights of Labor in the Catholic Church, which officially condemned secret societies. Much of the Knights' secrecy was dropped when Terence Powderley became their head in the United States, but more conservative bishops and priests still regarded it with deep suspicion. There were rumors that the pope was going to issue a condemnation of the organization, even though it had thousands of Catholic members.

Terence Powderley heard of the danger, and he went to see Cardinal Gibbons of Baltimore. Gibbons was a liberal-minded person. Also, he realized that in the United States the working people were very close to their Church, unlike the working class in some European countries. He felt that papal condemnation of the Knights of Labor would be a serious mistake, but he needed to know facts to prove to Pope XIII that the Knights should not be condemned as a secret organization. Powderley showed the Knights' constitution and by-laws to Cardinal Gibbons, which proved to the Cardinal that the Knights were not against the Church or their country.

In 1887 Cardinal Gibbons sent a letter to the pope in which he described the organization and its good work to help laboring people. Pope Leo XIII was convinced by the Cardinal's letter, and no condemnation of the Knights of Labor came. In fact, the pope now began to have talks with workers and employers from France and other countries.

26. Gradually, many people realized that industrial workers were being treated unjustly. Individuals— bishops, priests and ministers, lay people, factory owners—tried to help with social programs. Also, a group of intellectuals studied the problem and reported on their findings. Leo XIII followed the studies closely, and he published an important encyclical on the condition of working people. This encyclical *(Rerum novarum)* offered guidelines for correcting labor injustices.

The growth of industrialism from the end of the eighteenth century on certainly enriched society. But it also brought a series of new problems: industrial unemployment and crowded cities, and population problems. Only gradually did some sensitive people realize the seriousness of these problems and try to find solutions to them. Some went in for individual, personal action; others tried to begin social or political projects.

Roman Catholics, too, participated in this work. Social action and social programs grew in European Catholic circles in the decades of the sixties and seventies. We have already mentioned the work of Bishop von Ketteler and Father Adolf Kölping. Another figure in Austria was Baron Karl von Vogelsang, who tried to promote cooperative associations of workers which would improve conditions without resorting to class conflicts. In France

there was the amazing industrialist Léon Harmel, who organized his textile factories in such a way as to encourage worker participation in decision-making and management.

There were intellectual developments as well. Men like Bishop Mermillod in Switzerland and Joseph Toniolo in Italy formed study groups, and the members of these groups did important research into various social questions. Leo XIII closely followed these studies; he had taken note of the difficult situation of industrial workers when he was the papal nuncio in Brussels. When he became the bishop of Perugia, he wrote a pastoral letter on the whole subject. In it he acknowledged the contributions made by industrialism, but he also urged that greater attention be paid to the needs and value of human persons.

Supported by the advice of Toniolo, Leo XIII decided the time had come to deal once again with the whole subject. In 1891 he published an encyclical entitled *Rerum novarum (On the Condition of Working People)*. It quickly came to be seen as a great papal document that laid the foundations of official Catholic social thinking and offered guidelines for Catholics at work in this area. The encyclical offered a moving description of the terrible situation of workers and indicated that such a state of affairs could not be permitted to continue. Leo XIII proposed a fairer division of private property, greater government involvement in the social question, and associations of employers and workers.

The encyclical attempted to apply traditional Catholic teaching to the conditions brought about by industrialization. A main concern was the strengthening of the family. Besides wishing to help working people, Leo XIII wanted to head off the extreme forms of socialism, which were anti-religious and often inhuman. The pope was also very concerned about maintaining peace in the world. Labor unrest would lead to violence, he feared.

Rerum novarum was a serious first effort by the papacy to put the influence of the Church on the side of industrial workers. It made some important points. In particular, it made clear that economic principles alone were not enough to set society aright.

27. After the publication of the papal encyclical *Rerum novarum,* Catholic efforts in social action for workers increased all over Europe. However, some people thought that the Church was interfering in a matter that was not its concern. They did not understand that social action was a way of applying the gospel message to daily life.

Around the same time an important movement began to make its influence felt among Protestants in the United States. It was known as the Social Gospel movement. Such men as Washington Gladden (1836–1918) and Walter Rauschenbusch (1861–1918) vigorously stressed the social implications of Jesus' message. They tried to point out that Christianity did have something to say about social problems. The prophets of the Old Testament and Jesus himself had said things which related to the problems of the poor in the growing cities of America, to fair wages, and so forth. This movement certainly gave new voice to strains of American Protestantism which went back as far as the early Puritans in New England. And, interestingly enough, the movement stressed some of the themes which have recently been heard in Latin American liberation theology.

It should also be noted that serious religious influences were present in the Populist movement among rural Americans. ("Populist" means "of the people.") This movement at one point hoped to unite farmers in the South and West with industrial workers in the East.

The papal encyclical *Rerum novarum* (*On the Condition of Working People*) probably shocked some sectors of society, including some Catholic lay people and clergymen. Poverty and social injustice have always been with us, and to some people the Roman Catholic Church now seemed to be interfering in matters which were not spiritual. Ideas and attitudes from an earlier day continued to exist in some people's minds; they were not used to hearing the gospel message being applied to areas such as economics, government, and job conditions.

On the other hand, many Catholics were also inspired by the social concern of the encyclical and by its new ties with the gospel message. In almost every country in Europe, Catholics undertook social-action programs in the years following the publication of *Rerum novarum.*

In Belgium some priests went to work among the miners, and there was talk of worker priests (priests who took jobs in factories, for example). Democratic leagues, promoted by Catholics, helped to pass labor laws which showed a greater concern for fairness and social justice. In northern Italy journals began to discuss social issues, and Catholics promoted social programs. In southern Italy Catholics made serious efforts to foster and improve agriculture and to develop other natural resources. In Naples some priests envisioned living in community as poor people and sharing their goods. In France textile workers and other trade groups organized themselves, and various forms of credit unions arose in rural areas. In Germany, Catholic associations organized libraries for workers. The teachings of *Rerum novarum* could also be heard on the lips of Catholics in Holland, Poland, Austria, Spain, and England. Sometimes people organized Catholic unions and political parties; sometimes they brought Catholic principles with them when they joined existing unions and parties.

28. Thérèse Martin, a young Carmelite nun who lived and died in France during the last quarter of the nineteenth century, lived out her principle of doing good in childlike simplicity. She described her "little way" in her book *The Story of a Soul,* which became very popular and is still read today.

In Alençon (Normandy, France) there lived a devout Roman Catholic family. The father, Louis Martin, was a well-to-do watchmaker and his wife was a talented lacemaker. They had five daughters. The youngest, Thérèse, was born in 1873. The family was very religious, and three of Thérèse's sisters had become cloistered nuns by the time she was thirteen. At the age of fifteen Thérèse entered the Carmelite convent at Lisieux, where the Martin family now lived. Two of her sisters were in this convent. Thérèse took her solemn vows and led a life of prayer, work, and silence. She helped train novices, and she did such humble tasks as washing and ironing clothes. She came down with tuberculosis at the age of twenty-three; the disease spread throughout her body and caused great pain. Thérèse died in September 1897 at the age of twenty-four.

Her convent superiors had been impressed by her simple goodness and holiness, so they had asked her to write down the story of her life and her spiritual experiences. That book, *The Story of a Soul,* was published a year after her death, and it became very popular. It has been translated into more than thirty languages.

Thérèse's autobiography offered a simple message and example of doing good with childlike simplicity. The little Carmelite nun became famous in the Roman Catholic world, and popular devotion to her began to spread. In 1925 Pope Pius XI formally declared her a saint, and in 1927 he proclaimed her and Francis Xavier the patron saints of foreign missionaries. She is also known as Thérèse of the Child Jesus and as the Little Flower of Jesus.

What did Thérèse do? She pointed out a simple way to holiness. She herself called it the "little way," because it did not involve great deeds. In the spiritual life, she said, we remain children in God's hands. We must entrust ourselves to God completely and perform our simple tasks with humility and goodness. We are weak, but God is strong. God will love us and take care of us as surely as loving mothers and fathers take care of their children. We must tackle our work here and now, without worrying too much about the future.

Thérèse, like most Christian mystics in the West, saw her spiritual life as a job and a mission. She was ready to work, and she thought that her work would continue as long as the world lasted. Here are the amazing words she spoke a few weeks before she died, when she was an unknown nun hidden away in a French convent: "I know that my mission is about to begin, my mission to make people love the Good God as I love Him, to give my little way to souls. If my wish is granted, I shall spend my heaven on earth until the end of the world. . . ."

29. Among Catholics in the nineteenth century, praying the rosary and devotion to the Holy Eucharist were popular. Among Protestants piety and spirituality were lively. Protestant missionary work spread rapidly after 1850.

Piux IX wanted to strengthen devotion to the Holy Eucharist and encourage popular devotions among Roman Catholics; he himself was devoted to the Virgin Mary. Pope Leo XIII did much to confirm and recognize these trends within the Catholic Church. He established new liturgical feasts and gave approval to new religious congregations centered around certain devotions.

Leo XIII devoted encyclicals and other writings to the rosary. It was he who started the practice of dedicating the month of October to daily recitation of the rosary. Family recitation of the rosary at home began to grow in Catholic circles. However, Leo XIII cautioned against certain tendencies which exaggerated the place of devotion to Mary in the lives of Catholics.

Devotion to the Eucharist also grew as an individual and group practice. Toward the end of the nineteenth century, perpetual adoration of the Eucharist became a popular Roman Catholic practice. Catholics believed that Jesus Christ was truly and fully present in the Eucharist, and now it seemed proper to show respect and worship for that mystery by remaining with the Eucharist throughout the

day and night. People would arrange among themselves to spend a few hours before the Eucharist, so that someone would always be there. The practice became part of special parish programs and missions, and some religious congregations also were formed to carry on this practice.

Eucharistic Congresses (huge national or international gatherings for deepening knowledge of and devotion to the Eucharist) were another feature of this period. The devotion may have originated in Avignon, France, in 1876, when thousands of Roman Catholics gathered for processions and liturgical services in honor of the Eucharist. Marie Romisier did much to foster the movement and make it an international practice among Catholics.

Protestant piety and spirituality were also very much alive during the nineteenth century, which some historians have referred to as "the Protestant century." Various denominations grew rapidly, and missionary work spread widely, especially after 1850. In the Anglican Church there were discussions about the place of ritual in worship, and ongoing debates about reforms in the official prayer book. The Anglicans, especially those devoted to ritual, did remarkable works of social welfare in the slums of London and other great British cities. Spiritual revivals and renewed calls for study of the Protestant tradition took place time and again.

30. Novels became very popular in the nineteenth century. Writers modeled their stories after real life and explored the thoughts and actions of human beings. In England Charles Dickens described the lives of people amid the turmoil of the Industrial Revolution. In France, Honoré de Balzac wrote about middle-class people facing social changes. Painters, too, moved toward realism.

In the nineteenth century the novel rose to great popularity among Western readers. Its history can hardly be told here, but several points are worth noting.

Novelists now began to look at human beings and society in many different ways. In earlier writings, only upper-class people and royalty were treated as important characters, but now the poor and downtrodden, and also members of the middle class, were treated seriously and were sympathetically described. There was much popular storytelling of adventures and escapes, but novels also began to show their range as an authentic form of meaningful literature. Often published in serial form, they captured the imagination of readers from week to week and month to month. In England the endlessly creative Charles Dickens fashioned a whole world of unforgettable characters living amid the new industrial society. In France Honoré de Balzac spent night after night fashioning a picture of middle-class French people and their changing world. Only gradually did Christian thinkers and theologians come to realize that the world of the novelist and the fiction writer might offer serious food for thought.

There were also attempts to examine the Gospels as stories and to look at the writings of the Old Testament in terms of fiction and its techniques. The Bible was viewed as a varied work containing many different literary types. And some efforts were made to relate the story of the Gospels to the personal life and "story" of those reading the New Testament.

The turn toward realism, toward looking at the world outside as it really seemed to be, was also evident in the field of painting. A group of young French painters began to move out into the countryside and to paint the play of sunlight on the landscape as they actually saw it. Colors and outdoor scenes were used to show that what we looked at with our eyes was often vague, shimmering, and passing. In 1872 Claude Monet, one of the most typical members of the group of painters, produced his impression of a sunrise. A critic who did not like the painting and Monet's technique used the term "impressionists" to make fun of Monet's approach and those who followed it. And so these painters came to be known as the Impressionists. Some feel that the term "Illuminists" might have been better, since these artists were interested in the play of sunlight and how it "illuminated" objects.

Two other points are worth mentioning here. First, new trends in the arts often met severe resistance from those in official positions, especially those who led the artistic establishment, such as critics and older artists. People tended to remain attached to old ways of doing things, and to see new approaches as nonsensical or even dangerous. Second, a fresh look at reality may make the familiar world look less solid and real, may call into question one's old habits and beliefs. That kept happening as the nineteenth century went on, and it continued in the twentieth century.

In the nineteenth century there were some signs of spiritual revival and intellectual activity in the Russian Orthodox Church. The philosophies of Hegel and Schelling inspired some thinking in terms of idealism, and there was more attention to the writings of the Greek Church Fathers. Greek devotional literature was translated into Slavonic and Russian. Along with the Russian Bible, such literature provided much reading material for those Russians who could read. However, the vast majority of the Russian people could not.

There was also a revival of spiritual life in Russian monasteries. Some monks withdrew into lonely areas or huts to pray in poverty and silence. They became noted for their holiness and wisdom, and some were regarded as saints and miracle-workers. These monks, known as *startsi* ("elders") drew many people to listen to their simple message and receive spiritual advice.

Another spiritual notion in the Russian Orthodox Church was that of *sobornost*. It referred to a communion of minds and hearts among those who believe in Jesus. The union among them was a reflection of the oneness existing among the three divine persons of the Trinity.

31. The Russian Orthodox Church did not enter deeply into the lives of its people. Russian novelists, however, examined the part played by the Christian message in the lives of Russians.

The Russian Orthodox Church tended to be dominated by the government. It took little interest in social questions, such as living and working conditions for the poor. For this reason the Church was not respected by some intellectuals and others concerned about the plight of the Russian people. Russian theologians did not seriously study the meaning of life and the value of the Christian message in the changing world of the nineteenth century.

It was in the supposedly "secular" literature of nineteenth-century Russia that the deeper questions of human life and religious faith were powerfully expressed. Much Russian literature of the late 1800s dealt with the reality of the human soul and its inner life amid the events of history. Leo Tolstoy (1828–1910) is a famous author of this time. His works include *War and Peace* and many short religious stories—among them "Where Love Is, God Is." Deeply religious, Tolstoy called for a complete change in the Russian Church and State. His attempt to live a new kind of life among his peasants drew many visitors from around the world to his rural estate. He preached non-violence and simplicity of life, and he rejected all organizations which used force. But his view and practice of the gospel message were considered extreme by some officials of the Russian Orthodox Church, and Tolstoy was excommunicated in 1901.

Fyodor Dostoyevsky (1821–1881) turned from his liberal and Western beliefs to stress the Christian message and the mission of Russia and the Orthodox Church. In a series of astonishing novels he dove into the very depths of the human heart to probe sin and repentance (*Crime and Punishment*), the possibility of living a truly Christ-like life (*The Idiot*), the diabolical nature of rebellion (*The Possessed*), and a wide range of moral, spiritual, and religious issues in his final masterpiece (*The Brothers Karamazov*). The moral and spiritual earnestness of much Russian fiction is echoed in our own day by another Russian writer, Alexander Solzhenitsyn.

32. There was much debate and unrest in Russia as its people tried to find a way to modernize the nation and bring justice to the industrial and farm laborers. But the government developed a network of police to spy on people and keep watch on all activities. Most Russians were loyal to the government, but one group began to stress the importance of building a core of revolutionaries.

Russia was a huge country with its own striking features at every level. Peasants, who made up the vast majority of the population, were serfs until 1861. As serfs, they were something like slaves. They could not own their own land but had to farm the landlord's land. They could never leave their home farm.

When Czar Alexander II emancipated the serfs in 1861, it seemed to promise them a better future. But though serfs were now legally recognized as persons, they still had to pay certain taxes and could be punished by special rural courts. If they wanted to go away from their commune beyond a certain length of time, they had to get special permission. Thus, though they were freed from the iron authority of landlords, they remained bound to their local land in a number of ways.

The actions of the student population of the universities reflected the unrest in Russian life. From 1860 on, student protests, strikes, and acts of violence were a regular part of the Russian scene. The government

answered with mass arrests and deportations. While there were some crimes against the State, most of the population were loyal to the Czar, who was considered by the people to be their divinely appointed father. However, the Russian government developed a huge network of police to spy on the people and to keep close watch on all sorts of activities. Projects for economic growth and real advances went along in an atmosphere of suspicion and restricted rights.

How was Russia to grow and develop in the future? Various groups of Russians suggested ways. Conservatives firmly supported the existing Czarist regime and its traditional setup. Some liberals wanted to see changes come gradually. They hoped for a constitutional government and more liberal laws. More extreme liberals advocated a quick change to a new form of government, social reforms, universal voting rights, and a completely parliamentary form of government.

Another group was known as the Slavophiles, which included people of various views. In general, they felt that there was something special in the communal spirit *(sobornost)* of the Russian peasants. Slavophiles rejected capitalism and liberalism and wanted the peasants to be allowed to live on the land free of government interference. The Russian Orthodox religion, Slavophiles believed, was also very important in preserving the humanness of the Russian peasants.

Around 1898 the Social Democratic party was founded. From 1903 on, one section of it, the Bolsheviks, strongly advocated the theories of Karl Marx (1818–1883), a German social philosopher whose ideas underlie present-day Communism. The Bolsheviks' leader was Vladimir Lenin (1870–1924), who is known today as the founder of the Communist party in Russia, the leader of the revolution that overthrew the Czar in 1917, and the first Communist ruler. Lenin and his group worked to train revolutionaries who would use force and terror to destroy capitalism (the system in which private citizens own factories and businesses and produce goods and services). Lenin believed that the overthrow of capitalism would create a classless society.

33. At the Berlin Conference of 1884–1885, European countries, the United States, and Turkey met to discuss the opening of Western Africa. This conference led to the takeover of much African territory by European nations.

Until the middle of the nineteenth century European powers had usually been content to settle for commercial trading posts in Asia and Africa. Then the pace of competition and rivalry for national power and prestige quickened. Each country wanted to share in the economic spoils of the world and to extend its political power on the international scene. This desire grew as European explorers moved into the interior of Africa and began to open up West Africa.

In 1876 King Leopold II of Belgium set up an International African Association. It was supposed to fight the slave trade and help Christian missionaries in eastern and central Africa. More important, in the king's mind, were the agreements with various chiefs of the Congo region through his agent, Henry Stanley. By 1884 the basis of a very profitable colonial enterprise, to be called the Independent State of the Congo, was secure for Leopold. It was soon recognized by other powers, and Germany summoned an international conference to discuss the Congo issue and other problems relating to the expansion of European countries into Africa.

The measures agreed upon at the Berlin Conference seemed to promote free trade, attack the slave trade, and lay down rules for the takeover of African territory by European nations. But by the end of the conference much of Africa was destined to come under the control of one major European power or another. That control did bring some benefits to Africans, such as certain technical skills, education, and medical facilities. But the losses were great.

The takeover of Africa by various European powers was not a peaceful affair. In many areas African chiefs and their people put up fierce resistance, but they were no match for European weapons. There were local wars, uprisings, massacres, and executions. Thousands, perhaps millions, of Africans were killed in the whole process. Macemba, an African chief in southern Tanganyika, wrote to the invading Germans: "I have listened to your words but can find no reason why I should obey you—I would rather die first. . . . I do not fall at your feet, for you are God's creature just as I am. I am sultan here in my land. You are sultan there in yours. . . . I do not say to you that you should obey me, for I know that you are a free man."

The average Westerner who went to Africa brought along ignorance of that continent, false assumptions of superiority, and a host of other prejudices. A native African scholar, E. Bolaji Idowu, has pointed out how these uninformed and prejudiced opinions affected Western views of Africa's traditional religion. Most Africans believed in one supreme being, and they gave intermediate roles to other divine beings and to human ancestors. These were examples of beliefs on which missionaries could build in preaching the Gospel. Nevertheless, Europeans labeled these beliefs polytheism (belief in many gods), ancestor worship, and heathenism—terms that implied that African faith lacked true religious inspiration . Idowu maintains that Western use of these terms betrays Western ignorance and prejudice rather than real knowledge.

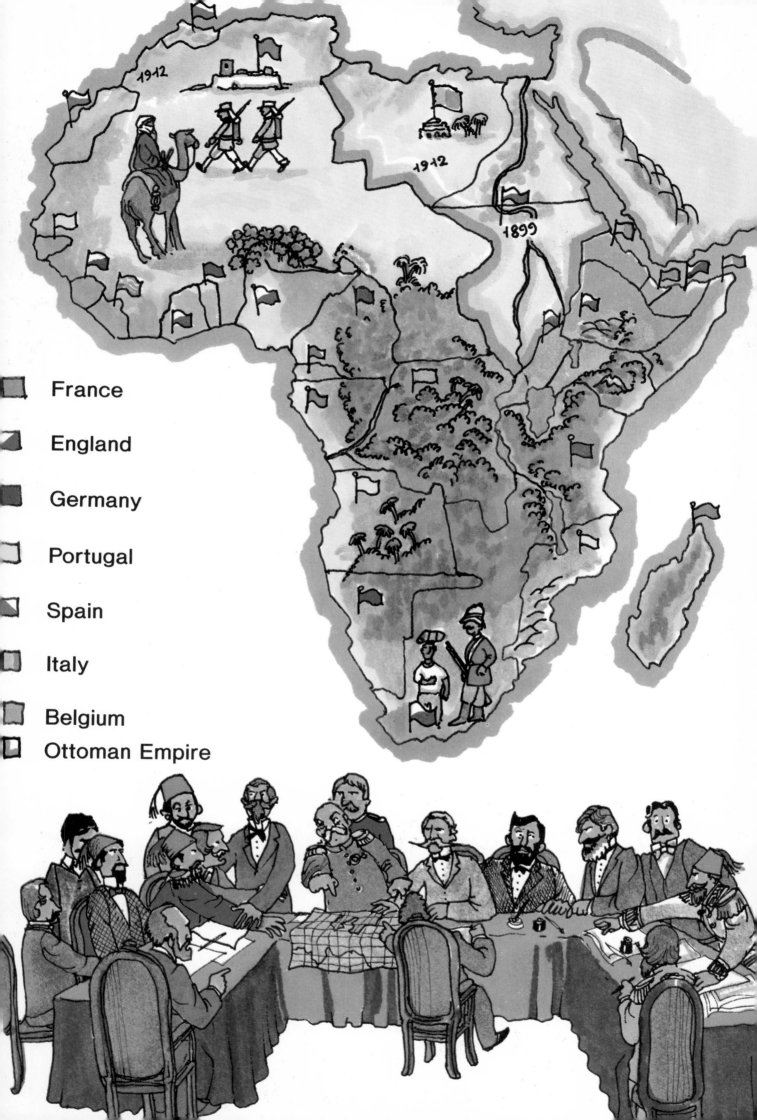

France

England

Germany

Portugal

Spain

Italy

Belgium

Ottoman Empire

34. Charles Lavigerie helped spread the teachings of the Catholic Church in Africa. He founded the White Fathers and the White Sisters and encouraged missionaries to live among Africans and come to know their way of life.

In 1867 Charles Lavigerie became the Catholic archbishop of Algiers. The country of Algeria had come under French control by that time and would remain so for a century. Lavigerie was made a cardinal in 1882, and two years later he was declared Archbishop of Carthage and Primate of Africa. His authority covered not only Algeria but also Tunisia and the Sahara.

In his very first pastoral letter Lavigerie addressed himself to Africans as well as European Christians living in Algeria. He hoped that his see would be a center from which Christianity could be spread to Muslims in Africa as well as to those who still held to traditional African religious beliefs. For this purpose he founded in 1868 a missionary society dedicated to Our Lady of Africa. Its members soon became known as the White Fathers and the White Sisters, from the color

influence Western governments on the issue, and he helped to get Pope Leo XIII to issue a letter against slavery in 1890.

Lavigerie was anxious to build a native African Church. He wanted to see African priests and catechists take over much of the work of the Church. He also was eager to send his missionaries and native Africans to Europe so that they could inform Europeans of the missionary work going on in Africa. Much more care was given to religious instruction before Baptism and to the native languages of particular areas. Thanks to the work of such groups as the White Fathers, there were about 2½ million Catholics in Africa by the end of the nineteenth century.

Another noteworthy clergyman in Africa was Samuel Ajayi Crowther, the first native African bishop of the Anglican Church in Nigeria. He had been captured and sold into slavery as a boy, then rescued by an anti-slavery British ship as he was being sent to America. He was educated in Sierra Leone and London with the support of the Church Missionary Society. He was ordained an Anglican priest and sent to Nigeria, where he spent the rest of his life in organizing missionary work and developing missions, schools, and other church activities. He himself translated the Bible and prayerbooks into Yoruba, and he helped to train many African ministers and missionaries. They lived and worked with the local population, exercising great influence on southern Nigeria. In 1864 Crowther was consecrated first Anglican bishop of the Niger Territories, and he died in 1891. By the end of the century there were about 2½ million Protestants in Africa.

of the clothing they wore. These missionaries were soon spreading to many parts of Africa. They crossed the Sahara, traveled south on the Nile, went to Zanzibar, and settled east of Lakes Victoria and Tanganyika.

Cardinal Lavigerie wanted missionaries to live with people of a given area and come to know them. The missionaries were to build schools and orphanages. They were to engage in needed social and charitable works as they went about the task of preaching the gospel message and introducing converts into the life of the Church.

The White Fathers were among the most dedicated opponents of slavery and the slave trade, which was still being carried on by some Africans as well as by Turks, and other Muslims. Lavigerie himself warned local authorities about letting the slave trade continue. He carried on a long campaign to

35. Among the Christian
witnesses in Africa were
Edward Blyden, a Black
Presbyterian minister,
and Charles de Foucauld,
a French Trappist.
Both were forerunners
of movements that would
grow in the next century.

One of the best-known and prophetic figures in Africa during the nineteenth century was Edward Wilmot Blyden (1832–1912). Born in the Virgin Islands of free Black parents, he lived in Venezuela and the United States before moving to Liberia. Blyden finished his education and theological training in Liberia and was ordained a Presbyterian minister. Highly intelligent and forceful in expressing what he knew and believed, Blyden became deeply involved in all phases of Liberian life over the next twenty-five years. He spent the rest of his life in Sierra Leone and Liberia when he was not traveling on lecture tours and government missions to various countries.

Gradually Blyden began to develop his own view of Africa and what the life of Black Africans should be. He began to make comparisons between the character and culture of Europeans and Africans. More and more he became convinced that Africa had a contribution to make to world civilization and that its contribution would be a spiritual one. As he saw it, the African social system was more

solidly grounded on cooperation, equal sharing, and a balanced community life than European society was. He strongly attacked European racism, materialism, and excessive reliance on science and industry at the expense of human and religious values. His oft-repeated message to Black Africans would be picked up by others in the twentieth century: "Your first duty is to be *yourselves*. . . . You need to be told constantly that you are Africans, not Europeans—Black men not White men—that you are created with the physical qualities which distinguish you for the glory of the Creator, and for the happiness and perfection of humanity."

A different sort of witness to the gospel message was given by Charles de Foucauld. A former officer in the French army, he underwent a deep religious conversion and returned to the Catholic Church in 1886. He became a Trappist monk, studied theology, and was ordained a priest in 1901.

Gradually he had come to feel that there was a special vocation for him in the East. In a letter to an old friend in 1901 he described it: "We want to found [establish] on the Moroccan border, not a Trappist house, not a big rich monastery . . . but a sort of humble little hermitage where a few monks could live . . . in penance and adoration of the Blessed Sacrament, . . . not preaching but giving hospitality to all comers, good or bad, friend or enemy, Muslim or Christian. It is evangelization not through the word but through the Blessed Sacrament, the Mass, prayer, penance, . . . [and] brotherly and universal charity that shares the very last mouthful of bread with any poor person, any visitor, any stranger, and welcomes every human being as a beloved brother." Such was the life he led, first in Béni-Abbès and then in Tamanrasset on the Sahara desert, until he was killed by bandit raiders on December 1, 1916.

Charles de Foucauld had no followers in his lifetime. But the publication of his personal papers inspired the founding of the Little Brothers of Jesus in 1932, the Little Sisters of Jesus in 1939, and related associations of priests and lay people in the 1950s. They continue his kind of gospel witness around the world today.

36. David Livingstone, a medical missionary and explorer, is famous for his reports on Africa and its people. Also important at this time was the growth of Christian churches in such areas as New Zealand and Australia.

Probably the most famous missionary of the nineteenth century was David Livingstone (1813-1873), the Scottish medical missionary and explorer. With the support of the London Missionary Society he undertook important explorations, traveling thousands of miles in southern and central Africa between 1841 and 1873. Livingstone's attitude toward Africans was far better than that of many other Europeans. He was deeply interested in Africans and their beliefs. He hated slavery and its bad effects on African life. His reports on Africa and its peoples were important and valuable, particularly since he had seen so much of that continent. For example, he explored the Zambezi River from the Indian Ocean to its source and came upon Victoria Falls and Lake Nyasa.

The missionary spirit of the Christian churches in the nineteenth century was amazing. Much of the work was of course less exciting and less known than that of Livingstone. But solid, important work that built up church life was being done in many areas by both clerical and lay missionaries. The progress made in Australia and New Zealand is a case in point.

Australia began its modern contact with the West as a penal colony for British convicts. After the middle of the nineteenth century, however, most of the immigrants were free people who had come there on their own. The White population came from Great Britain and Ireland. The Anglican Church (with the largest number of members) and most of the Protestant churches of Great Britain were soon represented in Australia. By 1914 there was much talk about cooperation among various Protestant churches in carrying on mission work and providing theological education. There was also talk about the possible union of various churches.

The Roman Catholic Church in Australia was made up largely of Irish people. The work of earlier priests and missionaries began to bear fruit with the growth of dioceses and church organizations. By 1910 there was a flourishing church life, and bishops were holding councils regularly. The first National Australian Catholic Congress was held in 1900. Patrick Moran was made archbishop of Sydney in 1884 and a cardinal and following year.

White settlement of New Zealand, too, came from Great Britain and Ireland, and church growth there in the nineteenth century was in many respects similar to that in Australia. Between 1860 and 1920 New Zealand's population more than doubled, and that of Australia increased almost five times. Both Australia and New Zealand, particularly the latter, were leaders in social reforms and democratic practices that came only later elsewhere. Women's right to vote was recognized in 1893 in New Zealand, in 1902 in Australia.

37. The development of the "Y" in the 1800s promoted unity among Protestants by emphasizing that faith in Christ was the most important thing. At the same time, Lewis Wattson of Graymoor worked for unity between the Anglican and Roman Catholic churches.

Many Protestants in many countries worked to unite their churches. Two factors helped to foster this ecumenical movement (ecumenism). First, increased missionary efforts encouraged members of different missionary groups to work together. Second, there was a new enthusiasm for religion; it was called the evangelical revival. (*Evangelical* means "in the spirit of the gospels.")

Two groups which exemplified the revived religious spirit and helped to spread ecumenism were the YMCA (Young Men's Christian Association) and YWCA (Young Women's Christian Association). The Y's, as they were called, were very active in the United States after 1870. Their program of sports, social activities, and educational and religious activities showed young people in cities and colleges the supreme importance of faith in Christ.

John Mott (1865-1955), a Methodist and YMCA leader at Cornell University, was an important pioneer in the ecumenical movement. At his suggestion the World Student Christian Federation was founded at Vadstena, Sweden, in 1895. Mott traveled to many countries promoting this student movement, and from its ranks came committed Christian leaders who in turn encouraged cooperation among members of different Protestant denominations.

During this time, many people began to take part yearly in an eight-day period of prayer for the intention of uniting the Anglican and the Roman Catholic churches. This was the beginning of the Church Unity Octave, and its founder was Father Paul of Graymoor. Father Paul (Lewis Wattson) was an Anglican-Episcopal priest who founded the Society of the Atonement in New York in 1897. In 1907 Father Paul began the Church Unity Octave. These eight days of prayer began on the feast of St. Peter (January 18) and continued through the feast of the Conversion of St. Paul (January 25). Father Paul and his community became Roman Catholics in 1909. The Church Unity Octave was approved by the pope and today continues to be celebrated in January.

Burghaus

38. Around the end of the
nineteenth century,
millions of people left
their homelands to look
for better places to live.
Many went to North and
South America. Some were
extremely poor, and
others just wanted to find
more profitable work.
Many were Catholics who
brought their faith
to their new country.

Near the end of the nineteenth century it was difficult for many European peasants and craftsmen to live decently in rural areas. The fields and the woodlands of the countryside would not provide them with what they needed or wanted. Hence many looked for work and a better life in the cities.

Many families chose a different course, however. They left their homeland, crossed the ocean, and found a new life in the Americas. European immigration to North America had begun in the 1600s, and now it spread to South America.

We can imagine a family in the German state of Bavaria who made this second choice. The father was a woodsman who wanted a better life for his wife and children. This particular family was Roman Catholic, and their parish priest blessed them before they left their home village at the foot of the Alps and set out on their journey. On the coast of Belgium they boarded a ship with many other emigrants, all of whom were bound for Brazil. The emigrants were not all extremely poor. Some simply wanted to find more profitable work in a new land. Although the ship was crowded, the voyage had pleasant aspects, and people managed to make new friends.

When the ship docked in Brazil on a hot, sunny day, our imaginary Bavarian family found themselves in a very different and unfamiliar landscape. Rio de Janeiro was growing into a large city, and people from many lands filled the streets. Our family had the names and addresses of fellow Bavarians now living in Rio de Janeiro, so they did not feel totally alone. The father was excited but dignified as he walked through the streets. The Catholic churches helped them all to feel somewhat at home, and amid the sounds of the Portuguese language they could also hear other European languages.

Latin American Catholicism was fed by continuing streams of Catholic immigrants, who tried to maintain their old traditions. Even when contact with the homeland was lost, the practice of Roman Catholicism remained firm because it was shared by other segments of the Latin American population.

But the situation of the immigrant was not always as pleasant as that of our imaginary Bavarian family. Many immigrants arrived without money, contacts, jobs, or knowledge of the local language. Sometimes individuals arrived alone, having left their families and relatives in Europe. They were forced to lead lonely lives, often finding shelter in some dirty, unhealthful room or apartment.

For example, about 10 million Italians emigrated from Italy to other countries within one period of a hundred years. They were willing to accept any sort of work contract or to do any sort of work. They helped to construct the Trans-Siberian Railroad. They harvested grain in Argentina. They tended vineyards in Tunisia. They were lumberjacks in the forests of Brazil. They worked on streets of New York as knife-grinders, shoeshine men, and fruit vendors.

89. Some religious men and women worked among immigrants, helping them in every way possible. Frances Xavier Cabrini was such a missionary among the Italian immigrants in the United States. She is sometimes called the "Citizen Saint."

Churches and dedicated individuals were often the main source of comfort and aid for the newly arrived immigrants.

One truly outstanding figure was Frances Xavier Cabrini (1850–1917), the immigrant saint. Born in Italy, she became a nun and in 1880 formed a new religious order of nuns: the Missionary Sisters of the Sacred Heart of Jesus. Over the next seven years she established seven houses for the education of young people.

In 1888 Mother Cabrini went to see Pope Leo XIII and discussed her mission. He persuaded her to work among the Italian immigrants in the United States, even though she had always wanted to go to China. In 1899 she arrived in New York, and a little later she opened an orphanage for the children of Italian immigrants.

Though living in a foreign land and suffering from bad health, Mother Cabrini had amazing faith, will power and energy, and her achievements are astounding. She founded nurseries, schools, orphanages. She crossed the ocean twenty-four times in the course of her work. She traveled by ship, train, stagecoach, and mule. She created centers in New York, New Orleans, Chicago, Denver, Seattle, and Los Angeles as well as in Argentina, Brazil, Spain, France, and England.

Mother Cabrini had a sound business sense. She made wise investments with the money which came as charitable contributions. She did not hoard the money but used it for good works. For example, she started a hospital in New York, so that sick immigrants would have a place to stay. She rented two houses, bought ten beds, and started taking in patients. Her nuns slept on the floor. At the start she only had enough money to pay the rent for one month, and she still did not have the medicines and the medical supplies she needed. But from that shaky beginning would come Columbus Hospital. Mother Cabrini also wore herself out for the miners of Colorado and the inmates of Sing Sing prison.

In 1909, Mother Cabrini became an American citizen. She died in Chicago in 1917, and twenty-nine years later, in 1946, Pope Pius XII declared her a saint.

40. The way people lived, traveled, and communicated was being greatly changed by major discoveries and inventions. Just as important were new scientific theories, such as Einstein's theory of relativity.

There were scientific discoveries and technical inventions throughout the nineteenth century, but around the turn of the century certain discoveries and inventions began to revolutionize people's way of living in the world and viewing it.

New forms of transportation and communication appeared one after another: the gasoline motor (1888), the automobile (1891), and the airplane (1903); the telephone (1876), moving pictures (1894), and the wireless telegraph (1895). The discovery of X-rays in 1895 and of radium by the Curies in 1900 offered new possibilities to medicine. Electricity began to come into everyday use and transform cities and homes.

Just as important and revolutionary were some basic scientific theories that altered our way of looking at the world. Around 1900 several people rediscovered the work on heredity and genetics that had been published by Gregor Mendel, an Augustinian monk, in 1866. His careful experiments on garden peas, for example, showed how certain characteristics were inherited. His work also exerted great influence on the breeding of plants and animals.

Another theory published in 1900 was the quantum theory of Max Planck (1858–1947).

The basic idea was that energy was sent out and taken in by things in separate little units or bundles (called *quanta*), not in an even, continuous way as had been imagined earlier.

Then, in 1905, Albert Einstein published his theory of relativity. Stated very simply, his theory showed that time and space were relative to many systems, not absolutes existing on their own. Gradually a new picture of the whole universe as an ongoing process of matter or energy amid relationships led to awesome discoveries and further mysteries.

41. Between 1870 and 1900 the population of Europe increased greatly. Cities grew larger, but the population of rural areas stayed the same or dropped as people moved to the cities to find work. Urban life was often hard because cities lacked modern facilities. Also, most cities needed social reforms and more honest, efficient government.

During the last thirty years of the nineteenth century, the population of Europe increased by almost 32%. Even though the rate of births began to drop around the same time, the death rate dropped much faster. By 1900 one quarter of the world's people lived in Europe. It was the smallest of the major continental areas, but it was also the most industrialized. In 1900 there were ten Europeans for every four a century earlier.

The growth of towns and cities was one of the major results of this increase in population. The number of people in rural areas remained the same as it had been or else dropped. Fewer workers were needed to provide food for the growing population because farm machinery made the work easier. Many peasants found themselves getting poorer and poorer. People left the countryside to find steady jobs in the city, to enjoy the attractions of urban life, and to better themselves in many other ways. Married women persuaded their husbands to leave the land, and

young women left on their own to find a more interesting life. Anyone who urged poor people in city slums to return to the land and its more peaceful way of life went unheeded.

Towns and cities had their problems. In smaller ones, a certain company or employer or family might control much of the power and life of the community. Amid a seemingly peaceful atmosphere, as in the illustrations of this chapter, workers were often subjected to improper pressure and enjoyed little freedom. And there were often serious problems in the areas of disease, public health, housing, and work conditions.

In big cities, such as those of the United States, there certainly were many problems. For example, by 1890 there were over 1.4 million people living on Manhattan Island in New York. Landlords squeezed as many rooms as they could into their tall, narrow buildings. Garbage piled up more quickly than it could be carted away. The coughing of tuberculosis victims could be heard in the dark, smelly hallways of growing slums. Crime in the slums was more than matched by crime in city government. The cry for urban improvements and reforms began to grow much louder.

In Europe, the rapid growth of cities outpaced the ability of the churches to provide for the people's need in religious services, education, and social programs. As a result, many of the urban poor in Europe were alienated from Christianity. In the United States, however, and among Catholic immigrants especially, the city parish became a center of life for the poor working class, and the Church helped immigrants or their children ease their way into American life.

4·JULY·1776 PHILADELPHIA

42. Cardinal James Gibbons was a dedicated spokesman for the Catholic Church in America. A loyal citizen of the United States, he wanted Catholics to take active part in public life. He championed labor causes, fostered the growth of Catholic schools, and supported the founding of the Catholic University in Washington, D.C.

Cardinal James Gibbons (1834–1921) of Baltimore provided outstanding leadership for the Roman Catholic Church in the United States during this period. Born in Baltimore of Irish immigrant parents, he was ordained a priest in 1861 and became archbishop of Baltimore in 1877.

In 1884, Gibbons presided over the Third Plenary Council, a national council or conference of American Catholic bishops. The Council made many decisions that influenced the lives of American Catholics. Among these were the decisions to establish Catholic parochial schools, to provide seminaries for the education of priests, and to found the Catholic University at Washington, D.C.

In 1886 Gibbons was made a cardinal. Throughout his life, he was a dedicated spokesman for the Catholic Church and its teachings. He wrote a widely-read book entitled *The Faith of Our Fathers* (1876) that explained Catholic doctrines. Gibbons' attachment to the common people and their situation was shown in his famous defense of the Knights of Labor described in chapter 25. He often stressed the loyalty of Catholics to the United States and its democratic ways, stating that he would not change one word in the U.S. Constitution. Protestants as well as Catholics were his friends.

Gibbons was among those who wanted to see Catholics take an active part in every area of American life, without sacrificing their religious principles. He did not want them to remain isolated in little Catholic corners, fearful of the world around them. He fostered the growth of Catholic schools because, he said, Catholics had to be educated in their faith as well as in other subjects. He supported the founding of the Catholic University of America in Washington, D.C. Bishop John J. Keane was the University's first rector, and President Benjamin Harrison attended the opening ceremonies on November 13, 1889.

Four years later Cardinal Gibbons joined with the chief moderator of the Presbyterian Church to organize the Parliament of Religions at the Chicago World's Fair. These two American Christians discussed basic religious beliefs with representatives of other religions from around the world.

At home and abroad Gibbons repeatedly stated that democracy was a blessing for the Church. He certainly could point to the United States as one example. Despite inner disputes and outbreaks of anti-Catholic feeling, the American Church continued to grow. By 1900 there were over 12 million Roman Catholics in the United States.

(Note: For more information on the life and times of Cardinal Gibbons, adult readers will enjoy John Tracy Ellis's *The Life of James Cardinal Gibbons*. This superb two-volume work (and a condensation of it edited by Francis Broderick and published by Bruce in 1963) recaptures much of the history of the Church in America during these years.)

43. Isaac Hecker described Catholicism as a religion that fitted the American spirit and practices, and liberal bishops such as Cardinal Gibbons and Archbishop John Ireland liked his approach. When attention was called in France to Hecker's approach, it was misinterpreted and was labeled ''Americanism.''

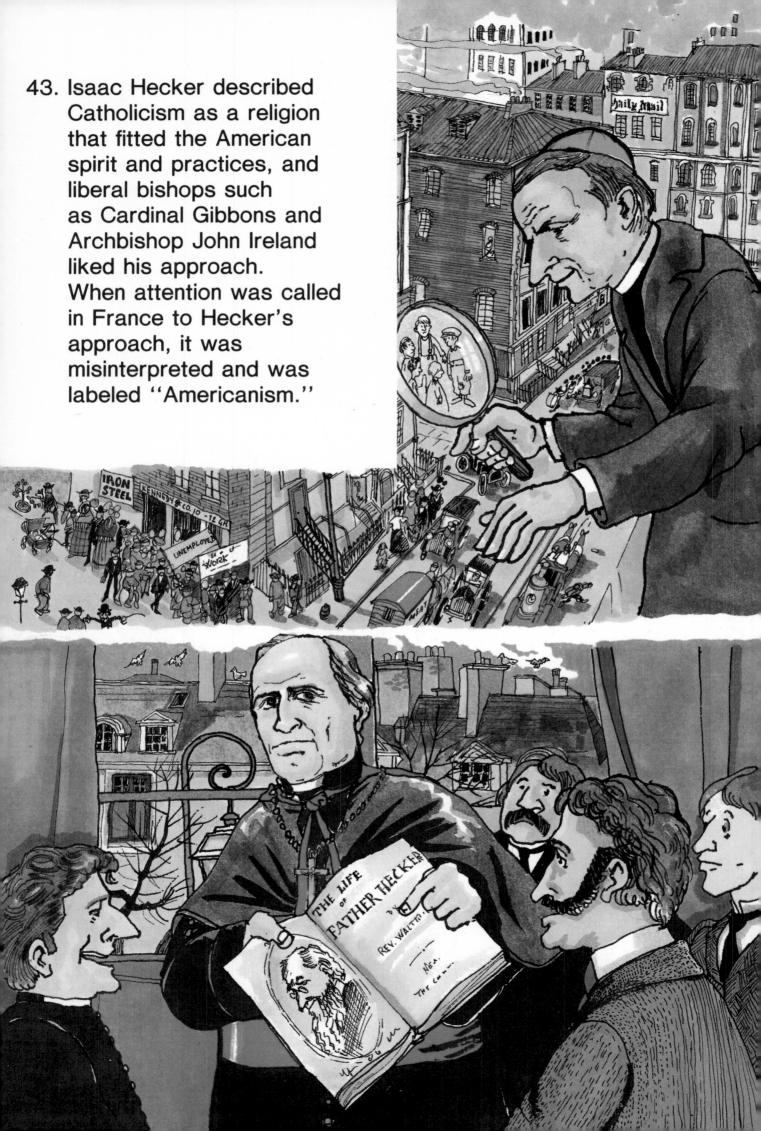

Isaac Hecker (1819–1888), American convert to Catholicism and founder of the Paulist Fathers, approached his ministry in much the same liberal spirit as Cardinal Gibbons. In a quiet but convincing way he pictured Catholicism as an answer to people's spiritual problems, an answer that went well with the ideals and practices of American democracy. He put much stress on active virtues, practical problems, and the workings of the Holy Spirit. But he was strictly loyal to the doctrinal teachings of the Church.

Some American Catholics, both lay people and clergymen, were suspicious of variations from the old way of doing things. When Archbishop John Ireland of St. Paul tried to find a compromise between parochial and public schools, such people were against it for fear it would endanger the faith. They did not approve of Cardinal Gibbons' having taken part in the World Parliament of Religions. Also, many German Catholics complained that the Irish-dominated bishops tried to Americanize them by doing away with the German language and culture of the old country.

A biography of Isaac Hecker was published in 1892 emphasizing his approach to the Church. Shortly thereafter, Archbishop Ireland visited France and praised Hecker highly. The French Church became interested in Hecker, and his biography was translated into French in 1897. Unfortunately, the translation was rather carelessly done and gave a wrong impression of Hecker's ideas.

An introduction to the book, written by a French priest, presented Father Hecker's methods as the correct way for the Catholic Church in France to proceed in the future. Some French Catholics agreed with him, but many disagreed. A conservative French priest drew up a list of views which he said were errors and which he attributed to Hecker. The French priest called these views "Americanism," and he said that Americanism was a heresy, or a teaching against the official beliefs of the Catholic church.

In France, in the United States, and among Catholics in many countries, the question of Americanism was argued. At the same time, a group of German-American Catholics prepared a list of complaints against the American bishops and sent them in a petition to Pope Leo XIII.

The pope rejected the petition. Then he appointed a commission to study the whole issue of Americanism. Not one American bishop was included on this commission. Finally, in 1899, Pope Leo XIII sent a letter to Cardinal Gibbons (*Testem benevolentiae*). In it the pope condemned various views about dogma, virtues, and church life which French conservatives had summed up under the term Americanism. The pope did not say that any American Catholics held these views, and he praised the loyalty and progress of the Church in the United States. Cardinal Gibbons wrote back that such views were no part of "our Americanism."

44. In Latin America there was conflict between liberals and conservatives. Liberals wanted land reform and separation of Church and State. Conservatives tended to support the Church. Often the government was under the control of the strongest person, regardless of the written law of the land. In Brazil, Pedro II was an outstanding ruler, and Brazil's products and population increased during his reign.

The situation of the Roman Catholic Church in Latin America between 1850 and 1920 was complicated, and its church members, who were spread out over a vast territory, came from all walks of life.

Many clergymen and religious faithfully tried to bring the gospel message to the people of Latin America, but a huge number of clergy were lazy and kept themselves apart from the people. Large landowners, including the Catholic Church and its bishops, were usually very conservative.

Liberals among the people were very anti-clerical and anti-religious. They believed in the philosophy of the Enlightenment, which claimed that people could arrive at truth through their unaided power of reason, with no need of revelation from God. Huge numbers of politicians were corrupt and enriched themselves instead of serving the people.

In many Latin American republics people lacked basic education and had no experience in self-government. Native Indians were often discriminated against by the white officials of both Church and State. Illiteracy, disease, and poor housing increased, and neither Church nor State did much to improve living conditions for the poor masses.

Liberals demanded land reform, separation of Church and State, and toleration of the various religions. When they came to power, they attacked the Catholic Church and its role in Latin American life. When conservatives came to power, they usually supported the Church and opposed all liberal measures. Strong men often took control of the government by force, disregarding the written constitution of the countries.

The situation, in short, was that the leaders of the Church thought the secular leaders wanted to destroy Christianity—and they did. The secular leaders thought the Church was too much involved in a wasteful, backward economic/social system—and it was.

One outstanding ruler in Latin American during this time was Pedro II of Brazil, who came to power in 1840. He was a constitutional monarch, ruling a poor country that had an uneducated population. Pedro encouraged education and industry. Coffee and rubber became important products. Railroads were built, and slavery was finally abolished in 1888. Pedro also favored religious toleration and freedom of the press, even when the press attacked him. But the Catholic Church did not like religious toleration, landowners did not like the freeing of slaves, military men did not like his strict control over their political activity, and some liberals now wanted a full republic. Pedro II was deposed peacefully in 1889, and a republic was established. During Pedro's reign, however, Brazil had steadily grown in produce, wealth, and the number of immigrants.

45. The work of Christian missionaries in China expanded greatly in the latter half of the nineteenth century. During this same time, Western nations often interfered in China's affairs.

Many courageous and dedicated Christian missionaries went to work in China during the latter half of the nineteenth century. One Protestant effort which deserves special mention was the China Inland Mission. It was created by James Hudson Taylor (1832–1905), who had grown up in a devout Methodist home. The China Inland Mission was supported by voluntary contributions and workers from any Protestant denomination. The mission made no efforts to establish mission churches. Its missionaries concentrated on preaching the gospel message, living among the people of the areas they visited, and trusting God for food and other needs.

Many Roman Catholic missionary groups were active in China, including the Lazarists, Jesuits, and Franciscans. Some 2,000 nuns, many of them Chinese, assisted in this missionary work. In 1918 these missionaries were joined by the Maryknoll Fathers, who were members of the Catholic Foreign Mission Society of America, created in 1900.

Unfortunately, many European missionaries were hostile to Chinese life and culture. Moreover, they did not want to give any real responsibility to native Chinese priests even though by 1914 there were some 700 of them. Some missionaries, including Vincent Lebbe, fought hard for a native Chinese Church, but they ran into stiff opposition from many of their European co-workers, and the Chinese Catholic Church was not entrusted to Chinese leadership until after World War I.

Christian missionary work in China was closely tied up with the internal politics of the country and the effects of Western imperialism. As European powers won special treaty rights and protected areas of their own in China, their citizens and missionaries gained freedom.

Many secret societies were formed in China to fight Western influences. The best-known society was the Boxers. Resentment against outsiders erupted into a massacre of foreigners and Chinese Christians in the Boxer Rebellion of 1900. Perhaps 16,000 Chinese Christians were killed. Eight nations sent a rescue force of soldiers to put down the rebellion, and those responsible for the deaths of Westerners were killed.

This powerful intervention from outside their nation helped to convince many Chinese thinkers and leaders that something had to be done about their weak Manchu government, which was headed by an emperor. A nationalist movement under Sun Yat Sen led to the resignation of the emperor in 1912 and the formation of the Kuomintang (National People's Party). Its aims were nationalism, democracy, and socialism. But civil unrest continued in China for many years.

46. After being closed
to Western nations for
several centuries, Japan was
opened in 1853 to trade,
diplomats, and Christian
missionaries. But in
spite of much hard work,
the number of converts
to Christianity was
disappointingly low.

Japan had been almost entirely closed to the Western nations for several centuries, but in the mid 1800s, Western commercial and political interests began to focus on Japan. In 1853 the United States sent several warships to Japan. This show of power forced that nation to reopen contact with the United States, and soon other Western powers were admitted into Japan.

Japan at that time had a decentralized government and faced many problems, but it was still a strong country. The people were united in their desire to reform their own government and in their dislike for Western interference.

The traditional theory and ideal of Japanese rule was that the emperor was the center of all life in the country. This ideal of imperial rule had seldom been reached in Japan, but in 1868 Japanese reformers restored the emperor to power. This restoration, which lasted from 1868 to 1912, was accompanied by one of the most remarkable and successful efforts in national reform during the past few centuries. Credit must be given to the Japanese people for their creative work in reforming their government and educational system, and in modernizing their country. This work of reform and modernization was combined, however, with loyalty to deeply rooted Japanese traditions.

In 1905 Japan defeated Russia in a war that made it clear to the Western world that Japan was a modern, powerful nation.

Despite persecutions, Christianity had remained alive in Japan since the time of Francis Xavier (1506–1562). In 1865 Father Petitjean of the Paris Mission had a truly moving encounter in Nagasaki. There he was approached by a group of loyal Japanese Christians who still followed old prayers, catechisms, and religious practices of the Roman Catholic Church. At that time there were

about 25,000 Roman Catholic Christians in the country. Gradually the legal prohibition against Christianity was dropped, and in 1889 religious toleration was granted. Leo XIII appointed an archbishop in Tokyo and established several other episcopal sees (dioceses). Both Leo XIII and Pius X were on fairly good terms with the court of the Japanese emperor. Other Roman Catholic missionaries came to join the members of the Paris mission, and American Protestant missionaries were particularly active. By 1914 there were about 70,000 Roman Catholics in Japan and 100,000 Protestants.

Nevertheless, the number of Christian converts was disappointing. Intense missionary activity, educational and social work, and publishing programs did not produce the results that had been hoped for. The native Japanese religious view, Shintoism, was strong and now revived even more. Missionaries often lacked sound knowledge of Japanese culture and of the people's way of looking at life. But the indirect influence of Christian ideals was very real. Christian schools did important educational work, Christian Japanese were national leaders, and there was growing interest among the Japanese in Christianity as a part of Western culture. Christian ethical ideals became a real factor in Japanese life, and many educated Japanese now knew more about Christian history and beliefs than they did about Buddhism, for example.

47. Giuseppe Sarto became pope in 1903 and took the name Pius X. He was a saintly man and also an effective, brilliant reformer. Unlike Leo XIII, though, Pope Pius X opposed untraditional views and religious approaches that dealt with the modern world. Pius X renewed the Confraternity of Christian Doctrine, the Catholic religious education program known today as "CCD."

The papal conclave which met after Leo's death in 1903 chose Giuseppe Sarto as pope. He took the name of Pius X.

Born of humble Italian parents, Sarto began to display his qualities of pastoral concern and spiritual leadership soon after he was ordained a priest. They became clearer when he was made bishop of Mantua: Within a few years Mantua had been turned into a model diocese. In 1893 Sarto became patriarch of Venice and a cardinal. He was already known for his able leadership, his personal holiness, his concern for priests, and his love for the poor. He was highly intelligent, hardworking, and effective.

As a church reformer, Pius X performed an astonishing amount of work in a relatively short time. One of his first concerns was to reorganize the Roman curia, the network of organizations in the Vatican which assisted the pope in his work. Pius X divided the curia into three main branches: Roman Congregations, which carried out tasks similar to those of a president's or prime minister's cabinet; church tribunals, which handled questions concerned with church law; and various offices, which handled the administrative work of the Vatican.

In a series of documents Pius X also dealt with the training of priests and seminary edu-

Congregations

Offices

Church Tribunals

cation. Smaller seminaries were to be combined, the program of study was to meet standards of public education in various subjects, and a year of studying philosophy was introduced into the seminary program. Newly ordained priests were also to be spiritually trained and dedicated, ready to serve their bishops with complete loyalty. Bishops themselves were now to make a trip to Rome every five years to report on their work.

Pius X also had a catechism prepared for the faithful. He used it in the diocese of Rome, and he urged its use in all the dioceses of the world. Every Sunday he himself explained the catechism to people present at papal audiences, and he never lost his pastoral interest in the common people. They returned his affection. Pius X also renewed the Confraternity of Christian Doctrine, a Catholic organization to teach religion. Today, in Catholic parishes in the United States, it is usually known by its initials, CCD, and is the counterpart of Protestant Sunday School.

Unlike Leo XIII, Pius X was firmly opposed to new intellectual ideas and trends in the modern world. He wanted to preserve the Church's traditional doctrines and practices from them, and he did so fiercely and uncompromisingly.

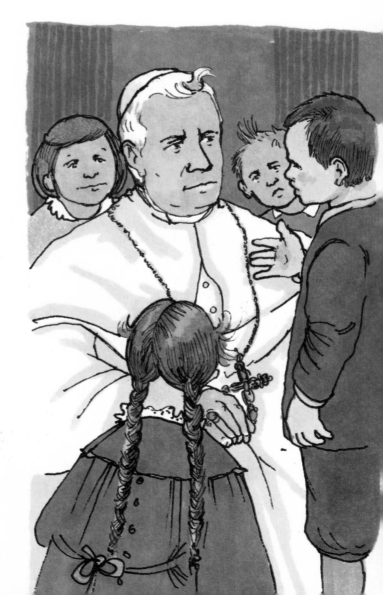

ACTA ROMANI PONTIFICIS

LITTERAE ENCYCLICAE

SS. D.N. Pii div. prov. PP. X ad Patriarchas, Primates
Archiepiscopos, Episcopos, aliosque locorum c
cem et s   onem cum Apostolica Sede
haben   de modernistarum doctrinis
A   TES ARCHIEPISCOPOS EPISCO
A   ORUM ORDINARIOS
PA   EM CUM APOSTOLICA St
               PIUS PP. X

Vener   tem et Apostolicam ben

Pascendi   Nobis divinitus
ficium id   ssignatum
tradit   stodia
pud   falsi
n   is
                     t

{PASCENDI}

Tyrrell

von Hügel

Loisy

Fogazzaro

Semeria

48. During the 1800s, some Christian thinkers tried to rethink the teachings of their churches according to the ideas of the modern world. This trend was known as religious Modernism, and it was condemned by Pope Pius X in 1907. In 1910 Pius X decreed that Roman Catholic priests had to take an oath against Modernism.

Throughout the nineteenth century there were sincere Christians who were anxious to relate the Christian message and the teachings of their churches to the modern world. Some other sincere Christians were opposed to any such effort. They feared that adoption of then-popular ideas in philosophy and history would undermine Christian teaching and practice.

In general, modernizing ideas won considerable acceptance among some Protestant churches, but in the Roman Catholic Church they met strong resistance, especially after the death (1903) of the diplomatic Pope Leo XIII.

We can only offer a few examples of modernist thinking in the Catholic Church during this period. In France, Alfred Loisy (1857–1940) was a Catholic priest and biblical scholar of exceptional talent. He wanted to relate the latest biblical theories to the traditional faith. In England, George Tyrrell (1861–1909), a Jesuit of Irish descent, did important work in the area of fundamental theology. He examined how the individual human being approaches God and religious truth. In Italy, Giovanni Semeria, a gifted Barnabite, did important work in the early history of Christianity before dedicating his life to children and war orphans. Another Italian layman, Antonio Fogazzaro (1842–1911), tried to relate Darwin's theory of evolution to Catholic dogma. He also published a novel, *The Saint,* which stressed the spirit of love at work in society and attacked abuses in the Roman Catholic Church. Encouraging and linking many of the Catholic Modernists was Baron Friedrich von Hügel, a loyal Roman Catholic who also remained loyal to many of his scholarly friends when they came under attack from conservative churchmen.

Conservative Catholics opposed to Catholic Modernism found a strong supporter in Pope Pius X. In a series of statements and actions he came down harshly on the movement. On September 8, 1907, he solemnly condemned a large number of propositions labeled Modernism. In 1910 he issued an anti-modernist oath which had to be taken by all Catholic clergymen. Some Modernists left the Church or were excommunicated. Most submitted to the papal decrees, and modernist thinking faded within the Church.

There is widespread agreement today that Catholic scholarship was seriously set back for some time by the condemnation of Modernism. This condemnation cast unfair suspicion upon Catholic scholars who, unlike Loisy and Tyrrell, fully accepted the Church's teachings. Conservative extremists used the word "Modernist" as a way of condemning those they disagreed with on matters of opinion. This situation continued until the death (1914) of Pius X and beyond. Modernism had been a serious threat to the Catholic Church, but the harsh reaction to Modernism also did much damage to the Church.

49. Some Protestant historians now recognized the influence of the Catholic Church in world history. Also, a number of Catholic writers—including Péguy, Claudel, Chesterton, and Belloc—defended the Church in their books.

Near the end of the 1800s, Catholic intellectual life revived in England. Gerard Manley Hopkins (1844–1889) stands out among the important writers of this period. A Jesuit priest, Hopkins was a major poet of Victorian England, though most of his poetry was not published until 1918 and after. He originated a poetic form called "sprung rhythm," which emphasizes the natural rhythms and sounds of words. His work revolutionized English poetry.

Other important English Catholic writers of this era are Robert Hugh Benson (1871–1914), Francis Thompson (1859–1907), and Alice Meynell (1847–1922). Somewhat later are Gilbert Keith Chesterton (1874–1936) and Hilaire Belloc (1870–1953). Chesterton, a poet, essayist, and novelist, is known for his brilliant style, full of paradoxes (statements that seem to be contradictory), his witty essays, and his ability to write humorously about serious matters. He is also remembered for his crime-fiction series featuring Father Brown, a wise and popular detective. Belloc wrote more than 150 books, including historical poetry, novels, and essays. His *Europe and the Faith* and *History of England* (the latter in four volumes) are well-known historical works. He often collaborated with his friend Chesterton.

In France during this period, Paul Claudel (1868–1955) and Charles Péguy (1873–1914) injected their concern for spirituality into all their writings. Claudel's plays reveal his mystical Catholicism, and he also wrote on the Bible. Péguy hated injustice passionately and had strong socialist ideals. *God Speaks,* an English translation of a collection of Péguy's

poems, is familiar to many English-speaking people. He is also famous for his poems on Joan of Arc.

Though among Roman Catholic writers, especially among converts, there was great enthusiasm for their church, to many Europeans the Church seemed out of touch with the modern world. Common workers in some European countries did not support the Church, and scholars often saw it as a relic from the medieval world.

However, there was also in Europe a new emphasis on historical study and tradition. Of great importance was the work of the Catholic historian Ludwig Pastor (1854–1928). His vivid, well-balanced sixteen-volume history of the papacy was his life work. Some scholars recognized the important role of the Church in European history and tried to present that role honestly. For example Leopold von Ranke (1795–1886), a Lutheran, emphasized the importance of the role of the Catholic Church and of the papacy in European history. In discussing von Ranke's work, Lord Thomas Macaulay (1800–1859), an English Lutheran, summed up the newer historical view in a famous statement: "There is not and there never was on this earth, a work of human policy so well deserving of examination as the Roman Catholic Church. . . . She saw the commencement of all the governments and of all the ecclesiastical establishments that now exist in the world; and we feel no assurance that she is not destined to see the end of them all. . . ."

50. Near the beginning of the twentieth century, revolutionary scientific views were matched in the arts and in other fields by revolutionary new ways of looking at reality. Some famous people of this time are: Freud, a psychologist; Nietzsche, a philosopher; Joyce, a writer of fiction; Klee and Picasso, painters.

As the twentieth century dawned, new ways developed of looking at human beings and at reality in many fields. Indeed, it was a period of revolution in the minds, hearts, and eyes of many creative people in the West.

In 1900 Sigmund Freud (1856-1939) published his *Interpretation of Dreams,* in which he explored the concrete, personal meaning of human dreams in a truly original way. By that time he had already worked out much of his new technique of psychoanalysis, in which patients talked freely, and then gradually came to see the connection between words, symbols, and personal problems.

In the very same year, 1900, Friedrich Nietzsche (1844-1900) died. His summons to develop one's human powers beyond the dull demands of social and national life had been phrased in the image of the "superman." Only in the middle of the twentieth century did a balanced picture of Nietzsche's meaning come from such scholars as Walter Kaufmann, an American philosopher of German and Jewish background. But in the meantime Nietzsche exerted a powerful influence on a wide variety of serious thinkers, such as Adolf Hitler.

The inner freedom and vision of the painter, sculptor, musician, and writer also became important around this time. In painting,

some artists began to move further and further away from merely picturing a scene as it might look to ordinary viewers and to portray how they themselves felt about it. They began to break up the elements of a scene and paint them as lines and shapes on different levels.

An important and widespread movement, Cubism, began with the arrival in Paris of Pablo Picasso (1881-1973), a young Spaniard, in 1904. His painting of the *Young Ladies of Avignon* (1906-1907) created a sensation. It did not present a single view of young ladies, but several views at once. Some of the shapes and heads of the young ladies were similar to features Picasso had seen in traditional African sculpture, which used geometrical shapes. By 1908 Picasso and Georges Braque (1882-1963), working together, had formed the style known as Cubism.

The same desire for personal freedom and for artistic expression of one's own vision and feelings was evident in the Blue Rider group of artists in Munich, Germany. Leaders in the movement were Franz Marc (1880-1916), Paul Klee (1879-1940), and Wassily Kandinsky (1866-1944). Kandinsky was a major spokesman who stressed the emotional qualities of colors, lines, and shapes and felt no need to paint pictures of things we see around us. Artists, he wrote, work out of their personal life, their emotions, and their spiritual vision.

The new way of sensing reality and of working as a creative artist was also evident in sculpture and music. Jacques Lipchitz (1891-1973) experimented with new geometric shapes to depict human figures in a more abstract way, but his skeleton-like figures were still human. In music, Igor Stravinsky (1882-1971) and Arnold Schönberg (1874-1951) rejected traditional melody and structured their compositions in new ways.

The same tendencies were evident in literature. Author James Joyce (1882-1941) developed the stream-of-consciousness technique and played with words to explore the whole fabric of human life. His famous books *Ulysses* and *Finnegan's Wake* demonstrate this technique. Around the same time, Marcel Proust (1871-1922) was exploring the links between time, eternity, memory, and experience in a human life. All life's impressions, he felt, were to be found in the artist's search for lost time. Or, as he put it in *Remembrance of Things Past*: "The only way to get more out of them was to try to know them more completely at the spot where they were to be found, namely, within myself."

**51. Early in the 1900s,
Pius X began work on a new
code of canon (church) law
for the Catholic Church.
During this same time,
emigration to the
Americas continued.
In Canada, immigration
was a major factor in
the growth of
Christian churches.**

The original European settlers in Canada had been French and Catholic. When the British government won control of the area in the eighteenth century, it tended to keep peace with Roman Catholicism for a variety of reasons—including political ones. The population of Quebec had always been overwhelmingly Roman Catholic. Catholicism also began to make some progress in other parts of Canada when Alexander Macdonell became bishop of Upper Canada in 1826.

Immigration was an important part of the settlement of Canada. The majority of the population was Protestant, mainly from England and Scotland, and the two main Protestant churches were the Anglican and the

In 1908 the Roman Catholic Church in Canada was granted normal status by Rome (that is, it no longer was considered a mission church). Catholics in Canada began to engage in widespread missionary work long before U.S. Catholics did. The Oblates of Mary Immaculate made heroic efforts to reach Indians and Eskimos in the North and West.

Catholics in Canada, as in other parts of the world, recognized the pope as their head and the city of Rome as the center of church authority. Many church officials were in favor of revising and updating the code of canon (church) law so as to have uniformity in its laws.

Piux X strongly favored this, and the work began during his papacy. By 1912 work was advanced enough to consult bishops around the world. The new code was finally promulgated in full in 1918 (though the new code still would not apply to Eastern Churches in union with Rome, which had their own system of laws).

Another revision of the code of canon law began after the Second Vatican Council, and was to be finished in the early 1980s.

Presbyterian. There were tensions between Protestants and Catholics over state aid for schools, and over other problems as well. There were tensions between French and English culture, between French and Irish Catholics, and between extremely conservative French Canadian Catholics and those of a more liberal attitude. The conservative character of the Church in France during the nineteenth century was also reflected in the French Canadian church.

52. While Pope Pius X was pope, there was growth in devotion to the Eucharist and in liturgy among Roman Catholics. Many Eucharistic Congresses were held in major cities throughout the world. Pius X also encouraged frequent Communion and lowered the age for children's first reception of the Eucharist.

Organizational reforms in the Catholic Church were not the only reforms as the twentieth century dawned. The devotional life of Roman Catholics began to resemble, in some ways, that of today's Catholic. Two noteworthy aspects of it were devotion to the Eucharist and participation in the liturgy.

Devotion to the Eucharist was encouraged by the many Eucharistic Congresses now held. Whereas France had been the homeland and center of these congresses for many

years, other countries now held national Eucharistic Congresses, and there were even several international congresses. In 1893, when a Eucharistic Congress was being held in Jerusalem, the pope sent his representative for the first time. Bishops of the Eastern churches that were in union with Rome were also invited to the Jerusalem congress to deepen unity between East and West.

Pius X was keenly interested in these congresses and hoped to involve the whole Catholic world by specifying where they were to be held. The pope was also eager to give them a more pastoral flavor. He used them and other approaches to urge the reception of frequent Holy Communion. He also led the effort to lower the age at which a child might receive Holy Communion. At that time, children did not receive Holy Communion until they were eleven or twelve years old. Pius X decreed that young children of six or seven might receive. He gave only two guidelines for deciding when a child was ready to receive the Eucharist for the first time: He or she should want to receive, and should understand that this Bread was not ordinary bread. He also emphasized that the Eucharist was meant to help people grow in their lives as Christians.

During this same period there were also many efforts to deepen the role of the liturgy in the lives of Catholics. The pioneers in these efforts were the Benedictines, who did special studies of a scholarly nature. Their translations of the Latin liturgy into the everyday language of people attracted great attention in Belgium and Germany. Gradually the congregation came to play a more important and active role in the Mass.

53. One of the great figures in the field of modern Catholic biblical scholarship was the Dominican Albert Lagrange. He founded the famous Biblical School of Jerusalem, which carried on archeological and textual studies. Lagrange was bitterly attacked and badly treated during the modernist controversy. But thanks to Protestant and Catholic scholars like Lagrange, biblical study became one of the great modern achievements of Christianity.

Much interesting work on the Bible was being done by Protestant scholars, and particularly by German scholars on the Old Testament. Julius Wellhausen's *The History of Israel* (1878) used a scholarly historical method to trace the development of the Hebrew religion and its worship of God. Many Protestants put up fierce resistance to such new views, but by 1890 the newer views were widely accepted in Germany.

Albert Lagrange, a Dominican priest, pursued studies in Vienna and sought to introduce the newer scholarship into Roman Catholic circles. A distinguished and highly respected scholar, he founded the Biblical School in Jerusalem. There scholars did work in archeology and on various aspects of the biblical text. Lagrange himself made many valuable contributions. After careful study of the first five books of the Bible, the Pentateuch, he challenged the view that they were written wholly by Moses. He came under sharp attack, and the Dominican Order demanded that he stop scholarly study of the Old Testament. Indeed, some of Lagrange's writings were put on the Index of Forbidden Books (though they were later removed), Lagrange was forced to leave Jerusalem for a while, and his journal (*Revue Biblique*) was almost put out of business.

For both Catholics and Protestants the Bible was a book inspired by God. How could it contain errors, if that were so? Yet scholars were finding errors in dates and in scientific matters, among other things. Extremely conservative Christians maintained that the scholars must be wrong, that what the Bible said had to be literally and exactly correct. Only later did many people accept the view that the important truths of the Bible were those which dealt with religious matters and with God's message of salvation, and that these truths might be expressed in terms of the world in which the biblical writers lived and the extent of scientific knowledge they had.

Under Pope Pius X this ongoing debate became a part of the whole modernist debate. Lagrange even wrote to the pope respectfully, expressing his loyalty but also questioning the reasons why most of his work had been totally censored. But it would be some time before the area of biblical studies would be healthily modernized.

In the area of biblical study Protestant and Catholic scholars have displayed an admirable spirit of ecumenism over the past one hundred years. Biblical scholarship, in fact, stands as one of the nobler efforts of the Christian mind and heart in the modern age.

54. Albert Schweitzer, the son of a Lutheran minister, became a famous organist, biblical scholar, philosopher, and medical missionary. In the early 1920s he built a hospital in French Equatorial Africa and then devoted his life to caring for sick Africans.

Albert Schweitzer (1875–1965) summed up in his own person and life much of the re-thinking that went on during the nineteenth and twentieth centuries. He was a philosopher, theologian, biblical scholar, professional organist, expert on Bach's organ music, medical doctor, and clinician in Africa.

In 1893 Schweitzer began his theological studies at the University of Strasbourg. He also found time to work in a nearby parish, preaching sermons and teaching catechism to children. In 1902 he was made director of a seminary, and he began a major study of biblical works dealing with the life of Jesus. His book *The Quest of the Historical Jesus* (1906) was a major work linking nineteenth- and twentieth-century scholarship. Schweitzer rejected liberal Protestant views of Jesus which pictured him as an ethical teacher of the modern European sort. Jesus, he said, lived in the world of his time and was deeply immersed in Hebrew ideas about the coming

end of the world and the establishment of God's Kingdom. Schweitzer's view formed a bridge between earlier and later work on Jesus and his life as an historical person.

Schweitzer's rejection of earlier liberal views did not mean he favored some conservative view of the Bible. Rather, he served as a link with the "theology of crisis" that appeared in Protestant circles during the early part of the twentieth century. But Schweitzer's views were not orthodox, and there was a clear linkup between modern Western humanism and religion in his life and work.

In 1911 Schweitzer received his medical degree. Two years later, with his wife Hélène Bresslau, he set out for Gabon in French Equatorial Africa. At Lambaréné he established a little medical center for the native population. Deported as a prisoner of war in 1917, he returned in 1924 to build a hospital and devote his life to caring for the Africans.

His interest was the "religion of love" and "reverence for life," not conversion of the natives to his beliefs. There, at the edge of the jungle, he also thought about the New Testament, the state of civilization, (Asiatic) Indian philosophy, and many other issues. His books on these subjects were widely read in Europe and North America. Schweitzer also described his medical work in Africa in a series of personal reports, the first of which was *On the Edge of the Primeval Forest* (1920).

Many people around the world were influenced by the life, work, and example of Albert Schweitzer. In 1952 he was awarded the Nobel Peace Prize. Deeply Christian, Schweitzer tried to follow the spirituality of Jesus, but he did not think that Jesus had all the answers for the problems of history. He felt that respect for the lives of all other beings was the key to a universal ethics.

55. Three people in India exemplified trends in Indian life and thought which deepened and spread right up to the present day. They are Ram Mohun Roy, who reformed Indian education and religious practice; Sri Ramakrishna, whose religious beliefs emphasized active charity; and Mohandas Gandhi, who combined holiness and political leadership in his own life and mission.

Three figures in India help to point up important trends in Indian life and thought which have grown and spread right up to the present day. Ram Mohun Roy (1772–1833), sometimes called the father of modern India, was an important reformer of Indian education and religious practice. Roy valued Indian culture for its higher ideals and its role in the life of India, but he was disturbed by the social backwardness of the caste system, discrimination against women, and other religious features which he felt were outdated. Roy was clearly influenced by Christian ideals. In *The Precepts of Jesus* (1820) he presented his own version of the ethical and humane ideas of Jesus. He founded newspapers in various languages to spread his liberal views. He wanted India to accept Western ideas so that it could become a modern state. In 1828 his organization called the *Brahma Samaj* ("society of God") began to exert great influence on Indian life among certain circles. Roy's attempt to renew the Hindu culture of India through Christian ideals and Western notions marked one strain of thought and practice that has continued down to the present day.

Sri Ramakrishna (1836–1886), originally named Gadadhar Chatterjee, was born into a poor Bengalese family in 1836. Around 1855 he began to center his Hindu worship around the goddess Kall, stressing her role as the loving mother of all humanity. After studying Islam and Christianity, he concluded that all sincere religions were useful ways to approach the Eternal. But he also felt that mystical union was the best way, if one could achieve it. Far from urging passive devotion, though,

Ramakrishna demanded that his followers engage in active charity toward others. Though Ramakrishna was not highly educated, his simple parables and way of living attracted many people. The spread of Ramakrishina's teachings was a part of the broader meeting between Eastern and Western religious cultures that became especially noticeable after World War II.

Mohandas Gandhi (1869–1948) became a lawyer in 1889, but he soon gave up his law career in South Africa to fight for the rights of his fellow Indians there. In 1907 he organized his first civil-rights campaign based on *satyagraha* (passive resistance). His campaign was successful, and he was a respected national figure in India when he returned there in 1915, where his greatest work still lay ahead. He stressed the unity of humanity under God, and he combined Christian and Muslim ethics with native Hindu teachings. He was remarkable for being an Indian holy man who united religious and political ideals in his daily life. This model influenced many people in the twentieth century.

56. World War I broke out in 1914.

As the twentieth century began, extreme nationalism became strong. The working classes, which socialism and other movements hoped to unite on an international scale, tended to divide along national lines. So did members of the various Christian churches, though they claimed to follow a universal message and to belong to a universal community.

Many nations stockpiled weapons, compulsory military service became common, and many civilians were involved in the business of military preparedness. The upper classes and some intellectuals, perhaps somewhat lonesome for old knightly ideals and uneasy with growing popular movements, tended to see war as one of the best ways to unify their nation and ensure its progress.

The French had not forgotten their defeat in 1871, and they wanted to take back Alsace and Lorraine from Germany. Italy wanted to take Trent and Trieste from the Austro-Hungarian Empire. The weakening of the Ottoman Empire and the growth of Slavic nationalism in various forms helped to feed tensions in the Balkans. Russia and the Austro-Hungarian Empire hoped to expand in that area, as did some other nations. Bohemians and Poles wanted independence from their present rulers. Outside Europe these same European tensions existed. Germany was challenging England for naval power, and

warring nations and to Roman Catholics. In a series of directives and pronouncements Benedict XV asserted that the Roman Catholic Church was completely neutral. Neutrality did not mean lack of concern, however. Catholics and all people of good will, the pope said, should work hard to bring about peace and to help soldiers and their families on all sides as well as civilians affected by the war.

Once Benedict XV had outlined a papal program, he faithfully carried it out. He tried to make contacts with the warring nations in order to stop the war. He urged Italy not to take part in it, and he sponsored all sorts of charitable works, without regard to the religion, nationality, or ethnic background of those helped. He made a deep impression on many statesmen, even those who had vague suspicions that the papacy was somewhat more favorable to Germany and her allies.

France and Britain, along with some other nations, renewed official relations with the papacy. Relations with the Italian government improved. In 1921 a statue in his honor was erected in Constantinople (Turkey) to celebrate all he had done for the peoples of Asia Minor during the war years. His peace proposals might well have served as a sounder basis for a new Europe than did the terms of the Versailles Treaty.

Benedict XV also gave a glimpse of new horizons in the area of mission work. In a series of documents he pointed out that mission work was a duty for all members of the Church, not just for volunteer missionaries. Newly founded church communities had equal rights with older communities, and they deserved to have their own native priests and bishops as well as their own culture.

59. The war ended with the Treaty of Versailles in 1918, but there was little hope for a lasting peace. Among Catholics in the years following the war, devotion to Mary, Mother of Jesus, grew stronger after her appearance to three young shepherd children in Fatima, Portugal.

When World War I ended in 1918, the peace-making efforts at Versailles were tragically undermined by some nations' self-interest, desire for revenge on the defeated countries, and poor statesmanship. Efforts to establish a League of Nations were defeated in the United States and undermined in Europe by lack of will power.

Our Lady of Czestochowa

Myslenice

Krak

What would the rest of the century hold? Of course nobody knew for sure, but there were isolated predictions and indications.

Back in 1872, as Prussia rejoiced in its victory over France, one great Swiss historian of Western culture saw the rise of new and terrible forms of rule. Jacob Burckhardt wrote ominously to a friend: "The military state must become one great factory. Those hordes of human beings in the large industrial centers will not be left indefinitely to their greed and want. What must logically come is a fixed and supervised share of misery, made wonderful by promotions and uniforms which begin and end every day to the sound of drums. . . . Long voluntary submission to individual *Fuehrers* and usurpers is what I see. . . . authority will again raise its head, a really terrible head, in the pleasant twentieth century."

While war was going on in Europe in 1916, a rebellion against British rule—the kind of rule that Burckhardt had spoken of—broke out in Dublin, Ireland, on Easter Sunday. The rebellion was crushed brutally, and many leading participants were killed. Within six years, however, a new and independent nation, taking in most of the island, rose in Ireland. The Irish rebellion was the first successful use of guerrilla warfare to win national independence in the twentieth century.

Devotion to Mary, the mother of Jesus, might seem to be a pious practice without social and political overtones. Twentieth-century events were to prove otherwise, however. This devotion had been growing among Roman Catholics throughout the nineteenth century. There were reports of appearances of Mary, and Marian Congresses were held from 1910 on. Then, in 1917, more visions of Mary were reported by three children in Fatima, Portugal. The apparition spoke of religious exercises in honor of Mary and Jesus, including recitation of the rosary and the reception of the Eucharist. There were also prophecies about the spread of Russian Communism, the outbreak of a second and more terrible world war, and the eventual conversion of Russia. Fatima became a place of pilgrimage, as Lourdes continued to be. When the war was over, pilgrimages to shrines of Mary increased again in Catholic areas such as Czestochowa, Poland. Indeed, the solid Catholic devotion of the Polish people would grow much later into many other forms of national solidarity.

Devotion to Mary was to have further implications and parallels in twentieth-century life. Many devout Christians would recall that Mary's bold prayer in the New Testament, known as the Magnificat (Luke 1:46-55), was rather activist and political in its overtones. It did, after all, speak of how God would cast down the mighty, raise the lowly, feed the hungry, and send the rich away empty. Many women in the twentieth century, as if responding to Mary's battle-cry, would speak out boldly for an equal place in religious and civil life.

Outline by Chapter

The Church and the Modern Nations
1850-1920

Chapters 18 and 19: Written by Marvin R. O'Connell
Chapters 20, 36, 41, 51, and 59: Written by John Drury